A Northern Union Man
The life of Harold Wagstaff

Robert Gate and Graham Williams

London League Publications Ltd

A Northern Union Man
The life of Harold Wagstaff

© The contributors: Graham Williams, Tony Collins, Robert Gate respectively.
Foreword © Harry Edgar.

The moral right of Graham Williams, Tony Collins and Robert Gate respectively to be identified as the authors of their contributions has been asserted.

Front & back cover design @ Stephen McCarthy.

All photographs are from private collections unless otherwise credited to the photographer or provider of the photo. No copyright has been intentionally breached; please contact London League Publications Ltd if you believe there has been a breach of copyright.

Front cover photo: Harold Wagstaff in a Huddersfield shirt in his prime; back cover photos: The 1914–15 Huddersfield team that won 'All Four Cups' and Harold Wagstaff in 1909 in an England shirt. (All courtesy Robert Gate)
The signature of Harold Wagstaff on the title page is a facsimile.

This book is copyright under the Berne Convention. All rights are reserved. It is sold subject to the condition that it shall not, by way of trade or otherwise, be lent, resold, hired out or otherwise circulated without the publisher's prior consent in any form of binding or cover other than that in which it is published and without a similar condition being imposed on the subsequent purchaser.

A CIP catalogue record for this book is available from the British Library.

Published in July 2019 by London League Publications Ltd, PO Box 65784, London NW2 9NS

ISBN: 978-1-909885-22-6

Cover design by Stephen McCarthy Graphic Design
46, Clarence Road, London N15 5BB

Editing and layout by Peter Lush

Printed and bound in Great Britain by Ashford Colour Press Ltd, Gosport, Hants PO13 0FW

This book is dedicated to the memory of David Gronow, Huddersfield rugby league historian and supporter, who sadly died in 2014, and is much missed by everyone involved with this book.

Foreword

Sport has always been a wonderful vehicle for the creation of drama, heroes and epic tales, and there is no doubt that every sport should remember those who built its history and created its legends. For the younger generation to fully appreciate their sport today it is important that they know something of what it once was and the people who built its foundations. This is especially so for rugby league which has a genuinely fantastic history of epic events and heroic figures, but which now seems happy to abandon so many of the things which made it great.

Most other sports would love to have the kind of back story rugby league has; indeed, some have successfully manufactured traditions with the help of smart marketing brains and a very supportive media. In contrast so much of rugby league's history has remained uncelebrated in a culture not given much to romanticism or recognition of the real value of its heritage. In fact – and this is something the modern world's marketing professionals would find unforgivable – rugby league actually killed off its own greatest tradition when, in the aftermath of the seismic changes to the game in the mid-1990s, it abandoned Lions tours and the Ashes Test series against Australia which had underpinned it for the best part of a century.

Alas, British rugby league has recently been bedevilled by too many people with a mentality of 'tradition doesn't pay the bills' and thus it has been left to a handful of independent writers and publishers to try and preserve the game's history and give due recognition to the people who did so much to create it. None are more deserving of such recognition than the men who represented our country on the international stage, and especially on Lions tours. There have been several truly outstanding Lions leaders, great men and great captains, but none who created such a revered place in the folklore of the game more than Harold Wagstaff, thanks to the way he led his country in its most glorious triumph of all, the 'Rorke's Drift' Test in 1914.

Of all the great figures in the history of rugby league no individual stands on a higher plane than Harold Wagstaff. His talents as a player would be enough to earn Wagstaff a place in any hall of fame, but he was much more – as a captain, a leader of men, and even a symbol of his sport as a then young and evolving game which was breaking down barriers, both on and off the field of play, in the years before the First World War. Wagstaff, with his fair hair and handsome features, was most people's ideal of what an England captain should look like – and he behaved with the dignity and high standard of sportsmanship such a position expected. His distinguished appearance and clean-cut looks set the benchmark for other great national team captains who followed, including Jim Sullivan, Gus Risman, Ernest Ward and Eric Ashton.

Yet, before the appearance of this book which you are now holding – published to mark the 80th anniversary of his death in 1939 – there has been no previous volume dedicated solely to telling Harold Wagstaff's story. He has remained a name known and respected by every rugby league follower with an interest in the game's history, but still very much a man of mystery. It is wonderful that now, thanks to the inclusion of a series of articles in contemporary newspapers and magazines written in Wagstaff's own words, much of this book has become an autobiography by the great man.

The publication of this book, compiled and researched by such knowledgeable and serious authors, is making a major contribution in preserving a very formative part of the history of rugby league in which Harold Wagstaff captained his country in its most epic triumph, helped build Huddersfield's legendary 'team of all talents' and played a major role in formulating new tactics and modes of play which shaped the game's future. It is also doing a great service to the history of British sport as a whole in telling the story of one of its greatest captains and most inspirational leaders.

Harry Edgar
Editor of *Rugby League Journal*

Acknowledgements

'*Ahr Waggy*' was originally published as a pamphlet in Australia; *Rugby League's Greatest Centre* series was originally published in *Yorkshire Sports Post*; *The Game I Love* was originally published in *All Sports Illustrated Weekly*; *Harold Wagstaff – The Prince of Centres* was originally published in *Rugby League Hall of Fame* by Robert Gate, published by Tempus Publishing Ltd (now The History Press) and is included here with their permission; *A Rugby Football Genius* is from *Great Games and Great Players* by V.A.S. Beanland; The Obituary and Funeral Report are from the *Huddersfield Daily Examiner*; *A Wagstaff Gate* is from *Rugby League Review*; and the articles on Leadership are from the *Rugby League Magazine* and *Rugby League Review*.

Thank you

Thanks to everyone who contributed material to this book, especially Graham Williams, Robert Gate, Tony Collins and Harry Edgar. Thanks to Steve McCarthy for designing the cover; the staff of Ashford Colour Press for printing the book and Millicent Christian for her assistance and support.

Because the autobiographical articles are a commonly used source of information about Wagstaff, there is occasional repetition in this book. We did not want to change the original pieces about Wagstaff that use these quotes.

Peter Lush & Dave Farrar
London League Publications Ltd

Contents

Part 1: Setting the scene   1
'Ahr Waggy'
Harold Wagstaff and the making of Anglo-Australian Rugby League culture
By Tony Collins

Northern rugby: A game forged under pressure   13
By Graham Williams

Part 2: In his own words   47

Rugby League's Greatest Centre   48
By Harold Wagstaff (from *Yorkshire Sports Post*)

The Game I Love
Or 15 years of Northern Union Football   121
Excerpts from a series written by Harold Wagstaff in *All Sports Illustrated Weekly* in the spring of 1921.

Part 3: Reflections on Harold Wagstaff   129

Harold Wagstaff – The Prince of Centres   130
By Robert Gate

A Rugby Football Genius   145
By V.A.S. Beanland

A Union man – Wagstaff & the NU Players' Union   150
by Graham Williams

Harold Wagstaff Obituary and Funeral Report   156
Huddersfield Daily Examiner

A Wagstaff Gate   162
Rugby League Review

Leadership   165
Rugby League Magazine and *Rugby League Review*

Appendix: Harold Wagstaff's playing record   166

Bibliography   168

About the authors

Tony Collins is Emeritus Professor of History at De Montfort University. He is the author of many books on the history of rugby league and the other football codes, the latest being *How Football Began: A Global History of How the World's Football Codes Were Born*, as well as hosting the weekly podcast 'Rugby Reloaded'.'

Robert Gate is a life-long rugby league follower, and has played a major role in recording and developing the study of the history of the sport. His many books include the ground-breaking *Gone North* (Volumes 1 and 2), *The Struggle for the Ashes*, his biographies of Brian Bevan, Neil Fox and Billy Boston and his study of the Rugby League Hall of Fame. He was formerly the Archivist at the Rugby Football League. He now lives in Wales.

Graham Williams, who lives in Otley, has been following both codes of rugby for longer than he sometimes cares to remember. A keen Leeds Rhinos fan for nearly 50 years, he developed an interest in the history of the game and from that made the leap to writing about it. Over the years he has had articles published in *Open Rugby, Code 13, Our Game* and *Rugby League Journal*.

In addition to articles he also authored or co-authored a number of books. Those for London League Publications Ltd have included *Rugby's Berlin Wall*, the biographies of Peter Fox and Mick Sullivan, *70 Years Reaching Forward* for Shaw Cross ARLFC and the *British Rugby League Records Book*.

Harry Edgar is the editor of *Rugby League Journal*, the sport's leading history magazine. Before that, he was for many years the editor of *Open Rugby*. He has also written various books on the sport and has made a huge contribution to preserving and developing the history of rugby league.

The plaque in Holmfirth opposite the Pump Hole from which Harold Wagstaff's first team took their name. Of the 12 plaques in the Holme Valley, this is the only one about a person rather than a place. (Photo: Peter Lush)

Part 1: Setting the scene

'Ahr Waggy'
Harold Wagstaff and the making of Anglo-Australian Rugby League culture
by Tony Collins

Northern rugby: A game forged under pressure
By Graham Williams

'Ahr Waggy'
Harold Wagstaff and the making of Anglo-Australian Rugby League culture

I'd like to start by saying what an honour it is to be invited to give this year's Tom Brock Memorial lecture. Among the small band of rugby league historians in Britain, Tom was a well-known and highly respected figure – so I hope that in some small way this lecture is in the way of being a tribute to the help and encouragement he provided to British historians over the years.

Certainly, I hope I'm more successful than other recent British rugby league visitors to Sydney – I note with trepidation that it's almost a year to the day since the pride of Great Britain flew into Sydney to take on Australia, only to fly straight back out again on the back of a 64–10 defeat [on 12 July 2002].

In such circumstances it seems downright perverse to ask a Pom to come and talk to an Australian audience about rugby league. In fact, the only thing I can think of which would be even more perverse would be to ask a Pom to come over to talk about cricket.

It's usual at events like this for the speaker to start with a few comments about his or her journey. Well, in the mental geography of the British rugby league supporter, the journey to Sydney is not very far at all; it's just a little bit further east than Hull.

Most kids growing up in a rugby league environment in Britain will know the suburbs of Sydney better than those of London. Growing up in Hull in the late 1960s, I could point out Penrith and North Sydney on a map of Sydney but I'd be hard-pressed to show you where Surbiton or Twickenham were on a map of London.

I remember when I was maybe 9 or 10, every Friday afternoon at school the teacher would give a pop quiz; she'd pick a letter and ask for the name of an animal, vegetable, country, town etc that began with that letter. One day she picked 'P'; when she asked for a town, I said Parramatta. "I've never heard of that, where is it?" she asked. "In Australia" I replied. "Are you sure you're not making it up?" she said. At that point one of my mates, a fellow Hull KR supporter stuck his hand up and said "Please Miss, I've heard of Parramatta". I'd like to be able to report that, just like in the movie *Spartacus*, all the kids rose one by one to declare that they too had heard of Parramatta. Sadly, they didn't, but the fact that at least three of us in the class had heard of it demonstrated what journalist Adrian MacGregor has described as the 'intangible bond' between rugby league in the two countries.

Which is what I want to talk about tonight. I want to look at how Anglo-Australian rugby league culture was formed, the parallels between the sport in the two countries and why the link has proved so durable. And I want to do that by looking at the career of possibly the greatest English league player of all, Harold Wagstaff.

Why Wagstaff? Wagstaff is crucial to cementing the link between Britain and Australia. He captained the 1914 and 1920 British touring teams to Australia and New Zealand, tours which established the template for future tours and he led Huddersfield's 'Empire Team of All The Talents', a side which heavily featured Australian stars as it swept all before it in the years immediately before World War One, in the process helping to establish the tradition of Australian players in the English league.

Just as importantly, he played a central role in the three key developments in rugby league that helped to forge a shared culture and identity for the sport in the two countries in the second decade of the twentieth century; namely, the development of a trade unionist, oppositional outlook among players, an innate sense of superiority over rugby union, and the contradictory combination of a working-class democratic spirit with loyalty to the Empire.

On top of the shared social circumstances of the rugby splits of 1895 and 1907–08, these developments helped to solidify Anglo-Australian rugby league culture.

Wagstaff's greatness was recognised by English and Australians alike. North Sydney's Sid Deane argued that Wagstaff was the difference between the two sides in the 1914 Ashes series: "Harold Wagstaff was not only brilliant in attack and wonderful in defence but his leadership was a most important factor in the team's success."

Dinny Campbell of Easts and later Norths described him as "the greatest tactician I ever played against. His personality was dynamic." *The Referee's* football correspondent, JC Davies, wrote about the 1914 third test, the so-called 'Rorke's Drift' test, that "Wagstaff, always a great player, that day became *the ubiquitous*, and the King of the game … Here, there and everywhere, all the time he was doing the work of half-a-dozen men. Wagstaff the Great." In 1946, seven years after his early death, the Sydney *Rugby League News* gave pride of place to Wagstaff's memoir of the 1914 series as part of its build-up to that year's test series.

As can be seen from these quotes, there is something totemic about Wagstaff, in his achievements, his reputation, almost in his very being. Even his name is quintessentially northern English. He was always Harold, not Harry with its connotations of princes of the English realm. The name almost seems to have be designed to emphasise the flat vowel sounds of Yorkshire and Lancashire. And of course, the aitch was rarely sounded – he was 'Arold, not Harold – a signifier of working-class speech in both the north and south of England. His nickname too, 'Ahr

Waggy', underlines the close and familial relationship he had with the game's supporters; in the north to prefix someone's name with 'Our' denotes a close family member, conveying, in the words of Richard Hoggart, a "sense of connection, of being part of a larger possessive whole, of not being only discrete individuals". In this, he parallels Gracie Fields, the singing star of the 1930s who hailed from Rochdale, and was known universally as 'Our Gracie'. (Incidentally, I'm informed by John O'Hara that in Australia this honour was extended only to 'Our Don' Bradman and the singer 'Our Glad[ys]' Moncrieff.)

"I am a Northern Union man all the way through," Wagstaff declared in the first sentence of a series of autobiographical articles published in 1935, 'and I was suckled in the Northern Union game'. He never played any other form of football seriously and did not even see a game of rugby union until he was in Australia on the 1914 British tour. He was born in 1891 in Holmfirth, a village now familiar to anyone who has ever seen the long-running BBC Television series *Last of the Summer Wine*. He made his debut for the local amateur side, Underbank Rangers, aged 14 and the following season scored their first try under the new 13-a-side, play-the-ball rules in September 1906.

Two months later he signed as a professional for Huddersfield, aged 15 years and 175 days, the youngest ever at that time. Two years later he made his debut in representative football for Yorkshire, selected to some extent because of his policy of not kicking the ball, a practice he continued to preach throughout his career, which eventually led to Huddersfield becoming known as the team which wouldn't kick, paralleling the great Souths sides down the years. A few weeks later he made his England debut against the 1908 Kangaroos. Eighteen months later, aged just 19, he was appointed captain of Huddersfield, a post he was to hold for the next 15 years. Aged 22, he was made captain of the national side.

The blossoming of his career matched that of the Huddersfield side. Crucial to that success were its Australian stars such as Glebe's Tommy Gleason, Newcastle's Paddy Walsh and, most of all, Easts great Albert Rosenfeld, who scored over 200 tries in just three seasons. Wagstaff's team finished top of the Championship table every season between 1911 and 1915, won the Challenge Cup twice and the Yorkshire Cup three times. In the 1914–15 season they won every trophy available to them, losing only two games in the entire season. They played the game in fast, open style that made the fullest use of the opportunities provided by the NU's rules, developing new tactics – such as 'scientific obstruction', the 'standing pass' and a hostility to kicking the ball – which moved the game far beyond the static set-pieces of its origins.

It was no accident that the metaphors and adjectives most commonly used to describe the team were those of science and industry, as exemplified by a 1924 description of the side: "There was an absolute understanding between all parts of a perfectly working machine which resulted in the most audacious and unexpected movements being carried out with a precision that left the opposing defence aghast. Fast and clever three-quarters were served by halves whose brains were ever working at high pressure behind forwards who, as occasion demanded, could play the traditional scrummaging game or convert themselves into temporary three-quarters and handle the ball."

For a town which had been built on the efficiency of its textile mills and spectators whose day-to-day lives were based on synchronised, collective working in those mills, Wagstaff's team was the embodiment of working-class industrial collectivity at play.

However, despite this iconic status and the high regard in which he was universally held, it is important to note that Wagstaff did not have an unproblematic relationship with the rugby league authorities, even after his retirement as a player. Indeed, the same can be said of many of Wagstaff's peers in the rugby league pantheon – of the nine players inducted into British rugby league's Hall of Fame in 1988, only the two Australians did not at some point clash with either their clubs or the RFL itself. This antagonism between players and officials came to a head shortly after the outbreak of World War One.

There has been a good deal of work produced in Australia on the War and the two rugby codes, such as that of Chris Cuneen and Murray Phillips. What is less widely known is that a similar, but not exact, division took place in England; union ceased operations in September 1914 while league carried on, although only unofficial competitions took place after 1915. More importantly, in November 1914, three months after the declaration of war, English rugby league was hit by a series of players' strikes opposing wage cuts which had been proposed by the clubs. Referees too threatened to go on strike.

The players were led by a four man committee, comprising Wagstaff, Gwyn Thomas, a Welsh full-back from Wigan who later joined Huddersfield, Charlie Seeling, the veteran New Zealander from Wigan who had toured Britain with both the 1905 union and the 1907 league All Blacks, and Leeds's Australian centre-threequarter, Dinny Campbell. The fact that the four leaders came from England, Australia, New Zealand and Wales – emphasising the international character of the sport in England – was also, consciously or not, highly symbolic.

Faced with a threat of all-out strike action, the rugby league authorities caved in and the compulsory wage cuts were rescinded. It is important to understand the context of these strikes – in the early months of the war there had been a huge hue and cry against professional football by large sections of the national press, much of it led by rugby union supporters, who believed that those who played or watched professional football were failing in their patriotic duty to volunteer for the army.

To go on strike for their rights as professional footballers was significantly out of step with the militarist hysteria which seemingly prevailed in Britain. Although there is no evidence of players explicitly opposing the war, their failure to completely fall in line illustrates the fact that pro-war hysteria was by no means the norm among sections of the British working class. It is interesting to note that the majority of league players only joined the Armed Forces after conscription was introduced through the back door in early 1916. And indeed, a recent study of the town of Huddersfield during the war has discovered deep levels of indifference and hostility to the war effort.

The so-called 'national unity' of World War One did not extinguish oppositional attitudes among players. In November 1920 Wagstaff and Gwyn Thomas were the two central figures in the formation of the Players' Union, the initiative for which had been generated on the 1920 British tour to Australia. For much of the next 18 months the RFL spent considerable time attempting to head-off the union's demands for higher wages, better benefits for players and a more equitable transfer system. The union's formation reflected the tremendous surge in class conflict which took place in Britain in the years following the end of the war. During this time Salford, Oldham, Barrow, Hull and Halifax all had to deal with threatened or actual strikes by players, and the union itself threatened two national players' strikes, although on both occasions it found itself out-manoeuvred by the RFL.

But by the end of 1922 the inexperience of the union's leadership, coupled with Wagstaff's health problems with a stomach ulcer and Thomas's somewhat abrupt flight to America, not to mention the divide and rule tactics of the clubs, led to the end of the Players' Union. However, it wasn't the last time that Wagstaff was to clash with the RFL – in 1929 he was initially refused permission to sit on the Huddersfield club committee because he was a former professional player.

Although British rugby league never had the same close links with the Labour Party that the Australian game had, the attitude towards the War and the deep divisions after it demonstrate a similarity of oppositional outlook that was shared among wide sections of both the Australian and British working classes. What's more, the cultural antagonism towards the southern English middle class archetype was also shared, in spades, by the northern English working classes.

This was most obviously demonstrated by the attitude shown towards the rugby union game by rugby league in both countries. Following the recruitment of most of the leading rugby league players into the Armed Forces in 1916, services union sides began grabbing them like kids in a candy store. The first significant match took place in April 1916 at Leeds when Wagstaff and three other league tourists were picked for a 'North of England Military XV' against an ANZACs XV, featuring Australians Tommy Gleeson, Newtown's Viv Farnsworth and Norths' Jimmy Devereux and Sid Deane. Despite never having played the game and seeing only one union match in his life, Wagstaff was the star of the match.

Later that year, Wagstaff, Albert Rosenfeld and half a dozen other league stars mysteriously found themselves all assigned to the same Army Motor Transport depot at Grove Park in South London, whose commanding officer just happened to be a member of the RFU executive committee. During the 1916–17 season, the Grove Park union team tore apart almost every other team in the south of England, including Australian and New Zealand services sides, winning 25 out of 26 games and scoring 1110 points while conceding just 41, setting a new British union record for points in a season. Their only defeat was a last minute 6–3 loss to a United Services side which included eight rugby union internationals plus Wigan's Billy Seddon and Leeds' Willie Davies. There was no secret to their success; as Wagstaff described it, the Grove Park team simply played "rugby league football under rugby union rules".

The record of the Grove Park team in the War, and to a lesser extent that of the similar Royal Navy Devonport side, firmly ended any lingering sense of inferiority rugby league supporters may have had in relation to union. In the eyes of rugby league and the communities in which it was based, rugby union, as in Australia, was quite clearly the junior code, less skilful, less athletic and much less satisfying for players and spectators alike.

This sense of superiority was underlined in the north of England by use of the everyday phrase 'best in the Northern Union', the implication being that if it was the best in the Northern Union, it was also better than anything else.

So, overlaid on top of the objective similarities in class and social circumstances of rugby league players in Britain and Australia, British players had also gone through experiences as club employees, as players in war-time and in rugby union which had given rise to attitudes and an outlook very similar to that of Australian players. Wagstaff himself noted that players of the two countries were noticeably more friendly – off the pitch, of course – following World War One. It is also interesting to contrast the relations between Australian and British league players with those in the union game.

The 1908 Wallabies were shocked at the level of snobbery they encountered and until the 1980s the British rugby union press had little positive to say about Australian players and tactics. Even as late as 1998, one of the reasons given for the sacking of Bob Dwyer as Leicester rugby union coach was the fact that he was 'too Australian'.

This could not be more different to league. Many Australian players who played for English rugby league clubs remained there after they had stopped playing. Albert Rosenfeld, who came over with the first Australian tourists in 1908, lived in Huddersfield until he died in 1970, working for most of his life as a dustman. The peerless winger Brian Bevan has a statue erected to his memory in Warrington. Arthur Clues, who made his reputation through ferocious assaults on the 1946 British tourists, settled in Leeds, becoming probably the most prominent of its sporting celebrities. When he died in 1998, the church had to close its doors because so many people wanted to go to his funeral.

A similar point can be made about many of the British players who came to play in Australia in the 1960s and 1970s and stayed on, such as Dick Huddart, Dave Bolton and Tommy Bishop.

This shared common identity could be seen as surprising given the ferocity and violence which were an integral part of Ashes test matches. The tone was set by the 1914 'Rorke's Drift' third test match – in which the two sets of players slugged it out to such an extent that at one point the British were down to nine players, yet still managed to pull off an amazing 14–6 victory, despite a second half which lasted 54 minutes due to stoppages for injuries. Six years later, the first test match between the two countries following the First World War set the tone for what was to come: "the contest was not characterised by anything striking in sportsmanship: that is, the striking things done were with fists or boots," wrote one reporter.

This intensified even more in the 1930s. The 1932 tour became notorious for the second test match, the 'Battle of Brisbane', which Australia won despite being reduced to 10 men at one point because of injuries, and both the first test and the match against the Queensland representative side were also characterised by fierce violence. Journalist Claude Corbett described the Brisbane match as "hard all the time, rough most of the time and foul frequently".

Nor did the experience of the Second World War do much to halt the violence; less than half an hour into the first test match following the war, Bradford school teacher Jack Kitching was sent off for punching Australian captain Joe Jorgensen. Clive Churchill's abiding memory of the 1948 Kangaroo tour to Britain was the violence of the English club sides. Bradford's Ken Traill described the third test of 1952, known as the 'Battle of Bradford', as the roughest game he had ever experienced.

Most notoriously, the 1954 Britain versus New South Wales tour match was abandoned by the referee just 16 minutes into the second half due to fighting. And the 1960s saw more players sent off in test matches than in any other decade, culminating in the 1970 World Cup final at Leeds, when vicious fighting between the players did not end when the referee blew the final whistle.

Yet such behaviour was never once used as a reason to question, let alone break, the relationship between the Australian and British rugby league authorities. This stands in marked contrast to the Bodyline cricket tour of 1932–33 when Jardine's bowling tactics appeared to threaten the future of Anglo-Australian cricket. Far worse misdemeanours than Jardine's were committed by British league players a few months before Jardine's men arrived in Australia without a hint of an international incident. Partly this can be explained by the importance of cricket to the Empire and the upper classes of society.

Yet, the 1932 test series created massive interest in Australia, being watched by almost 150,000 people, and press coverage, especially for the 'Battle of Brisbane' test, often moved from the back to the front pages of the newspapers. The opportunity certainly existed for at least the more sensationalist sections of the press to question the relationship between the two countries' rugby league authorities.

But this did not happen, due to two interconnected and contradictory reasons. Firstly, as we have seen, because of the deep cultural affinities between the predominantly working class constituency of the sport in the two countries. Secondly, and perhaps more controversially, the fact that Australian rugby league officials were as fundamentally loyal to the Empire as were their British counterparts.

In passing, I would argue that these were the reasons which also scuppered the 1914 and 1933 talks between the NSWRL and the VFL which discussed the possibility of forming a united nationwide Australian football code. The discussions came to nothing, partly because of differences over the rules but also, I would suggest, because a united game couldn't offer this combination of working class self-assertion and the imperial link.

The leaders of Australian league were extremely vigorous in their belief in Britishness. At a dinner in honour of the 1928 British tourists in Sydney, Harry Sunderland told the tourists to "remember Captain Cook; if he hadn't planted the Union Jack here, Australia might have become a Dutch dependency". "We are just as British as you are", protested Harry 'Jersey' Flegg, the president of the New South Wales Rugby League, in 1950 during a dispute with British tour manager George Oldroyd. "Australians look to England as the mother country in war, in industry and also in rugby league football," said Kangaroo tour manager ES Brown in an address to the RFL Council in 1954, explaining that "there is a strong desire to in Australia to get along with England from every point of view". When HV Evatt met the leaders of British rugby league in 1945, he argued that a tour to Australasia by the British was vital for "the best interests of rugby league football and of the Empire".

Just as importantly, it was the Australian press, far more than the British, which utilised imperial imagery for league test matches. It was they who dubbed the 1914 third test in Sydney as 'the Rorke's Drift Test', in comparison with the 1879 battle of Rorke's Drift during the Anglo-Zulu war, when 100 British troops held off 3,000 Zulu warriors.

In parentheses, it must be noted that a book published this year, *Zulu Victory* by Ron Lock and Peter Quantrill reveals that the British forces who relieved the troops at Rorke's Drift also massacred over 800 wounded Zulu prisoners in the aftermath. The battle of Rorke's Drift appears to have had special significance for Sydney; in 1882 the Art Gallery of New South Wales purchased Alphonse de Neuville's painting *The Defence of Rorke's Drift*, which you can still see prominently displayed in the gallery today. The use of such rhetoric continued even as late as 1958 when *Truth* began its report of the second test, again a landmark British victory against overwhelming odds, by quoting Shakespeare: "This happy breed of men, this little world … this England." Examples such as this, I would argue, also raise questions about the strength of Australian nationalism as expressed through sport before the 1960s.

But this loyalty to the Empire was also tempered with a hostility to many of the social mores of British society, especially its deference and class snobbery. Whereas Jardine, and English cricket captains in general until the late 1960s, were the embodiment of the English imperial elite, rugby league players manifestly were not. British rugby league tourists were not seen as representatives of a distant, and perhaps alien, government. In fact, they had far more in common with Australia's self-image as a country of the (white) working man than with the privilege and class discrimination that English cricket represented.

Much of the hostility towards Australia from the British upper and middle classes was based on a social snobbery which was also directed with equal venom at the working-class in Britain – "an entire continent peopled by the Lower Orders" in the words of English upper-class novelist Angela Thirkell. Jardine's tactics were unacceptable to Australians to a great extent because of what he represented. Yet physical intimidation and worse by a British rugby league side that shared the same social background and suffered similar frustrations as the great mass of Australians was a 'fair dinkum' part of the game.

Rugby league perfectly encapsulated the two seemingly contradictory attitudes of imperial loyalty but hostility to privilege. And Anglo-Australian test matches provided the arena in which both aspects of this relationship could be demonstrated. For many Australians and working-class Britons, the British rugby league tourists presented an image of the Empire in their own self-proclaimed likeness: working-class, democratic and meritocratic.

Made up workers from the industrial heartlands of Britain the British players were men just as they were. This sense of shared identity was sometimes reflected by the combatants on the field: when Nat Silcock and Ray Stehr were sent off for fighting in the first test match of 1936, they shook hands once they had left the field. During the 1958 Brisbane test Australian captain Brian Davies forbade his players from attacking British captain Alan Prescott's broken right arm (although this decision was heavily criticised by Clive Churchill among others). Most tellingly, following the 1954 abandoned match Britain versus New South Wales match, the players met that night at a dance and, according to Clive Churchill, 'had a good laugh' about the match – although Aub Oxford, who sadly died a few weeks ago, the referee who had abandoned the match, never refereed at that level again.

This leads to my final and perhaps the most important point about the significance of Harold Wagstaff to Anglo-Australian rugby league culture. Touring British rugby league sides were exclusively working-class – almost uniquely in comparison to any other sports' touring sides such as cricket or rugby union – and were captained and led by men who by and large worked with their hands when not playing football.

In an age when working people did not travel around the world – unless they were soldiers, sailors or emigrants, and then it was always under the command of their so-called social superiors – it was almost unheard of for a working class person to hold such a leadership position (outside of the labour movement). At best, a working class man – and the situation for working class women was far worse – could hope to be a trusted servant or the stereotypically loyal 'Tommy Atkins' character.

For working class Australians, just as much as British, to see a working class man such as Wagstaff as a leader of a British national side was an almost unprecedented event, which, along with his football skills, perhaps explains the tremendous coverage Wagstaff was given in the Australian press.

Wagstaff stood out as a symbol of what working people could achieve given the opportunity to get a 'fair go'. And it was rugby league which gave him, and many others from similar backgrounds, that opportunity. In the British army he would have been an NCO at best, but in rugby league he was a five star general. In short, he became 'Ahr Waggy' not just for English rugby league followers but for Australians too.

Wagstaff's memoirs of the 1914 Rorke's Drift test match were reprinted as much in Australia as they were in Britain – in 1946 the

Sydney *Rugby League News* gave them centre stage in its preview of the first Ashes test following World War Two, and as late as 1992 they were prominently featured in Geoff Armstrong's *The Greatest Game* compendium. One of the interesting points about the 1946 coverage is that discourse on the tour was wrapped up with the idea that rugby league was the most democratic of sports, as can be seen in this example from the *Rugby League News*. This was also repeated in Britain – the strength of the democratic ideal in league was (and is) very strong, beginning with the rationale for the split in 1895. British journalist Eddie Waring was a regular proponent of this view, and it was this sense that rugby league represented something more than merely sport which accounts for the fury of rugby league supporters around the world against Rupert Murdoch's attempt to take over the game in the 1990s.

I would like to end on a partisan note; after all, this is a lecture to honour a great supporter of rugby league and I have been proud to call myself a rugby league supporter since I was seven years old. The great Jewish novelist Isaac Bashevis Singer once noted that Yiddish had never been the language of a ruling class. A similar point can be made about rugby league: it has never been the sport of a ruling class in any of the countries in which it is played. Some see that as its weakness – on the contrary, that is precisely from where its strength is drawn. For without its deep roots in the working classes of the north of England and eastern Australia, the game would have survived neither the persecution of the rugby union authorities nor the corporate attacks of the Murdoch empire (nor, incidentally, its banning by the Nazi collaborators of France's war-time Vichy government).

It is this working class, democratic, 'battler' spirit – which is central to the sport in both Britain and Australia, and which is embodied in the career of Harold Wagstaff – that, to use a phrase that I believe that would be endorsed by Wagstaff, Tom Brock and countless others across Australia and Britain, has helped to make rugby league the greatest game of all.

This is the transcript of the talk Tony gave for the 2003 Tom Brock Lecture, an annual lecture held in Sydney in memory of rugby league historian and South Sydney supporter Tom Brock.

Northern rugby: A game forged under pressure

Harold Wagstaff, the future 'Prince of Centres', was born in the spring of 1891 in a village in the hills above Huddersfield. Even then, Huddersfield and the surrounding districts were in thrall to football in the winter months. Football there, like much of the north of England, was played under rugby rules and that was the game that Harold Wagstaff would be introduced to at an early age.

Growing up, another form of football, under Association rules, would attempt to grab his affection, but Wagstaff would return to rugby and embrace it as he grew into manhood. Those choices that affected him directly were part of a much wider drama that was being played out across the north of England. It was a period of flux and the northern rugby game, which he was destined to play so well, would experience difficult times and endure recurrent bouts of growing pains by the time Harold Wagstaff was ready for the world of work.

The rugby ascendancy that Harold Wagstaff was born into in England's northern counties was the result of a decade of solid endeavour across the 1880s. This had pushed the region to the forefront of the game in England and seen its influence impact on other parts of Britain. By the decade's end the northern region comprising the seven northernmost counties as they were then – Cheshire, Cumberland, Durham, Lancashire, Northumberland, Westmorland and Yorkshire – felt entitled to a certain swagger having popularised the RFU's County Championship and seen its strongest county – Yorkshire – dominate the competition from its inception.

Playing standards across the region had risen steadily and a growing number of northerners had found their way into the national team. Northern players had provided the vast bulk of the first touring team sent to the Antipodes and northern club attendances had largely underwritten the cost of bringing the New Zealand Native Football Representatives over to the British Isles. Those attendances in turn had put financial substance behind the Barbarian idea. One of the Barbarians' original opponents, Bradford, had become widely recognised as the region's strongest club thanks to its work in pioneering the three-threequarter game and bringing elements of scientific combination to the fore.

The game in the north was further modernised by the introduction of ground-breaking county-based league competitions in Lancashire and Yorkshire at the start of the 1890s.

At this time there appeared no reason why the northern region should not go on shaping the future of English – and by extension

British – rugby. Maybe that would have happened, but there were powerful forces standing in the way and beginning to bring pressure to bear on the northern game. Some of the old senior English rugby clubs, mostly southern based, but with influential northern supporters such as Liverpool and Manchester, wished to hold back the march of progress.

Other observers saw a threat to northern rugby's pre-eminence arising in central Lancashire. There the exploits of the Association game's leading professional exponents – Blackburn Rovers and Preston North End – in the FA Cup were grabbing lots of attention and making life difficult, if not impossible, for nearly all local rugby clubs. A few, but not too many, observers saw the north's position being made more complicated by the rise of the rugby game in Wales, something that seems to have caught English rugby by surprise. Why would that have been the case?

Ten years earlier, in mid-January 1882, the North was just starting to flex its growing muscular presence on and off the field. Although primarily an England trial selection, the North team was allocated a fixture against Wales. In front of 3 to 4,000 at Newport's Rodney Parade the North, fielding one England cap and five others who would go on to earn them, was strong enough to record a narrow victory over an inexperienced, but representative, Wales XV by a goal to a try. Even though defeated, Wales's strong showing helped to convince the RFU to put an end to regional opposition and for the Welsh to again be granted fixtures against the full England team the following season. It was a major step up in class and up to the end of that decade Wales's best result against England was a scoreless draw at Llanelli in January 1887. After that, England's dispute with the other Home Nations over the structure of the newly formed International Board ended fixtures for two seasons.

Things began to change once the 1890s got underway as the Welsh went on to record two early victories over England, at Dewsbury at the start of the decade and at Cardiff three years later. Atrocious weather meant there were probably fewer than 5,000 spectators present to watch the former at Dewsbury's Crown Flatt ground on Saturday 15 February 1890. That match which marked the resumption of fixtures also marked the first meeting between England and a Welsh team featuring four threequarters. Played on a quagmire in a storm of sleet and snow, the match produced just a single opportunist try from the Welsh half-back Bill Stadden who, in a sign of changing times, happened to be playing regularly for Dewsbury. When the following Tuesday's *South Wales Echo* ran a review of how the victory was reported in other newspapers it selected a piece from the *Leeds Mercury* which lavished praise on the Welsh performance: "The success of the [Welsh] team was due, however, to the brilliant and faultless play of the backs whose running, kicking, passing, and tackling has never been equalled in any of the historic games that have been played at Crown Flatt".

While a narrow victory over an untried England XV at Dewsbury would not have been seen as signs of real Welsh ascendancy, the appreciative reports in the press would have been very helpful in fuelling Welsh ambition to secure a leading role both on-and-off the pitch. A key element in advancing Welsh aims was a team that included four threequarters, two of them centres rather than the usual one. Its origins lay in Cardiff and it was at the city's senior club that the formation was developed in the early 1880s.

To be successful this attacking formation required a major shift in the way a team functioned. Previously on attack the nine forwards had always been the dominant element, often retaining possession for long periods while they attempted to subdue their opposite numbers. After Cardiff's reorganisation the balance would begin to shift. The now eight-man pack would have to accept a more subordinate role on attack, one of securing possession for their backs.

Under centre Frank Hancock's captaincy in 1885–86, Cardiff's intentions were clear; there was a huge emphasis on using the four-threequarter formation to promote attacking ball-in-hand rugby. His team soon showed its potential. After winning their seventh match at Llanelli by six converted goals and four tries to nil, the *Western Mail* on Monday 16 November stated that "the victorious team, not only should be the pride of Cardiff, but of the whole Principality, and strange it will be if their success does not stimulate to more scientific play the other teams of Wales".

By the season's end they had scored 131 tries but no drop goals, no penalty goals and none from a mark in their 27 matches. The possibilities of the 'passing game' had been laid out for all to see at the Arms Park. On the way to that almost invincible season, Cardiff had beaten four northern visitors – Runcorn, Liverpool, Dewsbury and Castleford – none of whom could put a point on the scoreboard. There might have been a fifth had Batley, the Yorkshire Cup holders, been able to add a fixture to their early season tour itinerary.

Missing Frank Hancock, who had retired, Cardiff took their four-threequarter formation on an ambitious five-day tour at the end of October 1886. The party set out on the familiar route to Moseley where a victory was secured. Next day the Cardiffians carried on northwards, past Birmingham for the first time. Liverpool was the first port of call where another victory was secured by two tries to nil. They then travelled on to their third and final match.

Word of Cardiff's prowess had spread beyond the cities to the smaller northern towns. It had been seen as a great accolade and a huge boost for a small town club's growing reputation that the 'Welsh Champions' had requested that their third fixture should be at Runcorn.

In front of 6,000 spectators on a wet midweek November afternoon, the home side excelled itself to win by one try and three minors to three minors. The following day's report in the *Western Mail* noted approvingly that "Runcorn who have administered the first defeat to the Welsh Invincibles are credited with being the best club met this year". For such an unfashionable club as Runcorn to be ranked so highly was wonderful publicity. A second northern journey, this time to Manchester, saw Cardiff play the return match with Swinton, another small town club in the process of building a reputation beyond the north, on 19 March 1887.

In frosty weather a very large Saturday crowd cheered the home side to victory by two tries and a dropped goal to nil. Cardiff's ground-breaking formation had hardly swept all before it on its northern travels, but that would in no way diminish public interest.

Meeting each other on the field was neither cheap nor easy. Money and time were needed to embark on what were often gruelling cross-country railway journeys. At a time when opportunities for most people to travel across Britain were rare, the overnight hardships were soon forgotten. What officials and players would remember would be the warmth of the welcome, closely fought encounters against some of Britain's strongest teams and the cordial atmosphere at social functions.

Enthusiasm for these fixtures was not confined to those on the pitch. When Llanelli journeyed to Liverpool in September 1886 the team was followed by three excursion trains well loaded with supporters. It was a popular rivalry that appeared to augur well for the future of both the English and the Welsh game.

At premier club level, four threequarters soon became the Welsh standard, but it was not until December 1888 that their national selectors felt comfortable committing to it. In doing so, south Wales became most closely identified with the new moves and different ways of playing being introduced to the game. WH Gwynne, the author of the chapter *International Football – Wales* in the Reverend Frank Marshall's book *Football: The Rugby Union Game* (1892) assessed the state of the game and complimented the Welsh saying that "In no rugby circle is the game pursued with such energy, assiduity and invention as in South Wales". Gwynne then went on to add that "The Welshmen have made up for their paucity in numbers by their science in play."

In keeping with the spirit of the times Welsh energy would make a massive contribution to the development of rugby as a technical game. That chapter did, however, recognise their weaknesses and English strengths, the author continuing by saying that defeat happened when the Welsh were confronted "by superior weight, strength and speed, which have broken down the system carefully planned and practised by the wily ingenious Taffs". There seemed little to find fault with in that view as it generally explained why English mass and momentum held the upper hand when the two teams met.

Reports of Welsh ingenuity fired the imagination in town and city alike. It led to Welsh ideas being readily adopted from the late 1880s onwards as more and more northern clubs overcame their scepticism and decided that they were clearly the way forward.

If the obstacles presented by the transfer laws could be successfully negotiated, the smart way to make a start was by importing one or two Welsh threequarters with first-hand knowledge to show in practice how things should be done. For the four-threequarter formation to work well, it meant showing just how the two centres should go about establishing a disciplined short-passing partnership.

Among the early ones willing and able to make the journey north were Bill McCutcheon, David Gwynn, Bill Keepings and Fred Cooper. Their impact on the clubs they joined, Oldham in the case of McCutcheon and Gwynn, Halifax in the case of Keepings and Cooper at Bradford, was hugely advantageous.

At representative level, mastery of the new formation took time. Except for Durham no other northern county had persevered with the formation and it was still clearly a work in progress when the North took on the South at Richmond on Saturday 17 December 1892. It had been expected that both teams would employ the four-threequarter formation, but injuries forced the South to take the field with the old three-threequarter line-up.

On the day, captained by one of the pioneers of the innovation in the region, Fred Alderson, the Hartlepool Rovers, Durham and England centre, the North XV failed to make the four-threequarter formation work. The South passed better, scored three tries and won 14–0. Not surprisingly, the England selectors stuck with the three-threequarter formation for the trip to Cardiff.

Three weeks later, the English XV made their first appearance at the Arms Park for the opening match of the International Championship. The Welsh campaign got off to a faltering start in front of a packed crowd of over 15,000. With a strong wind at their backs, the Englishmen coped with a slippery pitch better to score a converted try and a try without reply by half-time. When play resumed the Englishmen added the first of two more tries to their total. Arthur Gould, the Welsh captain, led his side's fightback. With the wind in their favour, the Welsh backs made full use of the space in front of them to run in three tries, just one converted, to leave them trailing by a single try. Defeat looked the most likely outcome until a last-minute penalty goal – the first ever kicked in an international – gave the men in red a historic first home victory. On the scoreboard victory might have been achieved by the narrowest of margins, but there was another equally important moral victory on the field.

As their lead shrank in the second-half, the English captain, Blackheath's Andrew Stoddart, had to pull a forward out of the pack to counter the threat of the seven Welsh backs. That victory seems to have convinced Gould, once a sceptic himself, of the value of the four-threequarter formation. Monday's *Western Mail* carried part of an interview given by Gould to a journalist from the *Morning Leader*. In it, Gould sounded the consummate professional as he considered his team's achievement: "English individual excellence far exceeds our own. With perhaps one or two exceptions we have no brilliant men; the whole secret of our success lies in our combination. We have thought that matter carefully out, and time is beginning to show that the four-threequarter system is the better one. We have not many clubs to choose our players from but that is not greatly against us, for we understand each other's play better and today we have vindicated the contention that combination amongst moderate players is superior to any amount of individual brilliancy."

Wales's next match was against Scotland in Edinburgh on Saturday 5 February. After a scoreless first-half the Welsh XV confounded the pundits, their spectacular running breaching the home side's well organised defence three times to win 9–0 and take a huge step towards their first Triple Crown.

After the match, Gould, a master propagandist for his nation's style of play, once again gave an interview to the *Morning Leader*. Once again, Monday's *Western Mail* carried part of that interview in which Gould said: "Our win was beyond my expectations. I think the moral effect of our victory will be to compel the Scots and the English clubs to play the Welsh style. The effect of this victory coming so soon after our own win over England will be to emphasise the merits of the new formation over all others. It will probably revolutionise the game, because once a set of players have thoroughly mastered the art, not only are they almost unbeatable by old-style players, but it is a thousand times more interesting to the spectators."

If Arthur Gould was right about Welsh style heightening spectator interest, and there were good grounds to back his view, then any organisations which relied on gate money had to consider if it was possible to make that style work for them.

There was no shortage of spectator interest in south Wales ahead of the crucial match against Ireland. Nearly 20,000 people were estimated to have crammed into Llanelli's Stradey Park in the hope of seeing history made on Saturday 11 March. They were not to be disappointed, although victory over the Irish was hardly spectacular, achieved by a single first-half try to nil. It was enough, however, for Wales and the four-threequarter formation to win their first championship and by virtue of their three victories claim the mythical Triple Crown, also for the first time.

Both the defeated Scottish and Irish captains questioned the four-threequarter formation's merits but just as Gould had predicted, Welsh success did compel the other three home nations to fall in line.

Enough of the leading northern clubs had made the change, as had Yorkshire, who were well on the way to retaining the County Championship, for the North XV's selectors to have another try at the four-threequarter formation. The meeting with the South was the most important rugby match to be played so far at an important new venue in south Manchester. Manchester Athletic Club had developed a new stadium out at Fallowfield and the trial was held there on Saturday 16 December 1893.

The captaincy of the North had passed to Heckmondwike and Yorkshire's outstanding threequarter, Dickie Lockwood. Under his direction the North got the better of the South by four tries to three, 16–9, in front of a crowd disappointingly below 6,000. As the trial's victors, the North team provided four of the backs and five of the forwards to an England XV which would face Wales fielding four threequarters for the first time. Confirming the North's ascendancy, Dickie Lockwood was recalled to the England team and appointed as his country's new captain.

The meeting of England and Wales was always scheduled for the start of January, which meant it was prone to being affected by bad – sometimes very bad – weather. At the start of 1894, the weather was very cold and the match at Birkenhead Park's ground was very nearly postponed. Overnight straw and a late thaw eventually saved the day, but the attendance once again was much reduced, 7,000 at most being present.

Many more should have been there, especially at a time when very few northern rugby supporters had first-hand experience of that 'revolutionary' Welsh style. Wales arrived at Birkenhead on Saturday 6 January with a team that showed just one change from the one that had won at Cardiff the previous year. There was little trace of that display as a poor disjointed Welsh performance offered little threat and a powerful performance by a majority northern pack allowed the English backs, well marshalled by Lockwood, to take full advantage.

On an icy pitch the English played brilliantly, outscoring the Welsh by four tries to one to win emphatically 24–3. That result, which the *Liverpool Mercury* emphasised was "not a beating – it was an annihilation", astonished the game's followers across Britain. Such a resounding victory left 'Welsh Athlete' stunned and he was forced to resort to blaming the outcome on poor selection and tactical blunders rather than the superior display of the English backs in his *Evening Express* column.

Still only 26, Dickie Lockwood looked to be the man to take northern rugby forward. That was until an inherent problem for northern rugby players, loss of earnings, kicked in. Ahead of the Calcutta Cup match at Edinburgh in mid-March Lockwood informed the England selectors he would not be available because he could not afford to take time away from his job. If he was hoping for a sympathetic response from the RFU and the Yorkshire Union he was to be very disappointed.

Disgusted by their attitude, Lockwood not only missed the match in Edinburgh, but announced his retirement from all future representative rugby. That only left his club, Heckmondwike, as the focus for his considerable energy and talent. Heckmondwike, however, was never a big enough club to be able to take on the great and the good of British rugby.

A move to Wakefield Trinity in October 1895 did not radically alter Lockwood's circumstances either; Trinity's playing roster was too thin on talent to provide him, as captain, with a real chance of carrying off the biggest honour in northern rugby. Lockwood had stepped away from the game's top-level at a crucial time and his leadership and tactical insight would be sorely missed.

Once again bad weather had kept the attendance woefully low when the Welsh XV had appeared in Birkenhead. There were probably many rugby supporters who hoped for better luck next time the Welsh team travelled north. Hardly any of those supporters at the time would have considered the possibility that it would never happen again. While they waited, those supporters wanting to keep up with news of what the clever Welsh, rugby's non-conformists, were doing with the game would have to continue to rely mainly on the sporting press.

What was read and sometimes heard would whet the appetites of the fortunate few who were able to watch a Welsh team in action. The chance came maybe twice or three times a year when a premier Welsh club or a county team representing Glamorgan or Monmouthshire would travel north.

In the early 1890s those premier teams seemed only to be appearing on the grounds of a few big northern clubs – Huddersfield, Oldham and Swinton – with any regularity. Of the visitors, Cardiff and Newport were particular drawing cards. To celebrate the opening of the newly extended Fartown ground at the end of October 1891, a leading club from each of the other most powerful rugby regions in Britain – London and south Wales – was invited to provide Huddersfield's opposition. Blackheath and Cardiff duly arrived. Despite being under strength, the Welsh visitors delighted the Saturday crowd of 10,000. According to the

Western Mail, the popular opinion was that "a better game had never been played at Huddersfield". Once the home team had reorganised to counter Cardiff's excellent back play, the match swung in their direction and they proudly claimed an opening victory, 16–8, at their revamped enclosure. When Cardiff again travelled northwards the following season, on 18 February 1893, this time at full strength, they took Swinton's unbeaten home record which had run for 12 months and in so doing became the first Welsh club ever to win there, 7–0. According to the local paper, "Swinton's backs were given a rare football lesson". Such regular praise only served to increase northern interest in Welsh rugby.

Newport, who were the pioneers of the development of forwards and backs co-operating in the loose, did not venture north in 1891–92. It proved to be a landmark season for the Usksiders, who remained unbeaten throughout, and at its end they were declared 'Team of the Season' by *Pearson's Monthly*. With that accolade and its £90 prize added to their standing, the Usksiders twice ventured north the following season. Known as a highly trained combination capable of fielding 10 Welsh internationals when at full strength, Newport scheduled matches at Swinton at New Year 1893 and then at Oldham on Easter Saturday. Such was the interest that at both Chorley Road and Watersheddings temporary stands had to be erected to cope with the demand. For the first time, Swinton made a match at Chorley Road all-ticket and had sold 15,000, leaving just 2,000 available, before match day. All Swinton's efforts came to nothing, however, as frost forced the cancellation of the match. Three months later, Oldham's committee was doubly delighted with a crowd of 14,000 and a home victory, 8–5.

The response to northern clubs, particularly Yorkshire ones, in south Wales was becoming less positive. In that part of Britain, heavy forwards largely reliant on physical strength to power their way through the opposition pack were dropping out of favour. On the same day that Newport was packing Watersheddings, Tyldesley on tour from Lancashire lost 5–0 at Llanelli. In his report of the match a correspondent for the *Llanelly Mercury* wrote "It was ever so with northern county teams. The English threequarters are nothing more than ornaments. The forwards are continually bent on keeping the ball hidden from view in a long and unending list of scrums. It is difficult to understand how football is so uncommonly popular in Yorkshire."

Considering its standing in the English game, Bradford had maintained little regular contact with the premier Welsh clubs. The *Western Mail* for Monday 26 February 1894 reflecting on Bradford's heavy defeat, 34–0, on their first visit to Newport at least gave the visitors some credit, commenting that "the game was contested in the best spirit imaginable and, though vigorous, there was an absence of the roughness with which Yorkshire games are, unfortunately, so much associated."

After Huddersfield had been defeated 6–5 at Rodney Parade on 6 October 1894, a *Western Mail* report commented that the visitors "True to their county traditions ... made it a forward fight" and then similarly paid them somewhat of a compliment saying that they showed "none of the roughness which some Yorkshire teams have displayed in south Wales".

The reputation of Welsh rugby now stood so high in England that Halifax, having successfully adopted a more attractive Welsh style of play, had inflicted some impressive high-scoring defeats on leading Yorkshire opponents in 1893–94. The club had every right to feel proud of the style of their play and the recognition it brought. Two of their threequarters – Fred Firth and Walter Jackson – had grabbed the attention of the national selectors and been chosen for the Calcutta Cup clash in Edinburgh while their young half-back Archer Rigg had been a travelling reserve for that match. Five weeks later, Halifax maintained its regional standing, retaining the Yorkshire Cup, scoring eight tries as they ran up a record score. Halifax's clever football at Headingley ought to have convinced many of the neutrals in the 16,000 crowd that the winners really were, as their supporters proudly asserted, 'the Newport of the North'.

A chance to watch Welsh style in action was eagerly anticipated. Cardiff's second of three scheduled visits to the northern counties in 1894–95 was to South Shields. Their ambitious hosts were striving manfully to become Durham's top club at the time and had built a reputation through fixtures with many of Yorkshire's leading clubs, nearly all members of the Yorkshire Senior Competition (YSC). Batley, challenging for honours in the YSC, had been there 10 days earlier and drawn "a good number of spectators" but Cardiff's visit there on 12 January was of a different calibre. According to the *Western Mail* report the hosts "regarded [the match] as the most important ever played there". A below strength Cardiff team won 8–3 on a cold wintry day in front of 7,000 spectators. In his review of the outcome 'Welsh Athlete' concluded that "The visitors, notwithstanding, gave such a brilliant exposition of the handling code as has never been witnessed in Tyneside district since the sensational defeat of the Northumberland cup-holders by Newport last spring."

The popularity and vision of the Welsh game meant its confidence was increasing just as northern confidence was being dented by the rapid rise of Association Football across the region. Association's growing presence in the mid-1890s was pushing rugby in the northern counties into crisis on-and-off the field. While the battle over payments to players for loss of wages, 'broken-time', raged in the press and committee rooms, the northern clubs were still largely pursuing their forward dominated approach while the Welsh style, which focused more on the backs, was drawing praise from critics across the British Isles.

Playing four threequarters had failed to revolutionise the game's outlook across the northern counties and the region was in real danger of being supplanted as the main challengers to the metropolitan leadership of the British game.

What then was the perception of the rugby game in England's strongest region in the mid-1890s? Some northern scribes detected a change in northern tastes. Reviewing the prospects for 1894–95 a journalist on the *Leigh Journal* could write "People prefer to see a league game even if it is all scrimmaging. League games rouse spectators and have virtually killed off ordinary fixtures, no matter how pretty the play." Northern rugby might have had the most extensive club and league structure, have big games that could draw crowds of 20,000 or more, and its leading county teams were the strongest in the country, but for all its popularity at home it did not seem to be generally appreciated abroad. While partly that was down to the well-drilled and uncompromising northern style of play, it was also partly because the northern clubs appeared pre-occupied off-field with finding northern solutions to northern problems.

That is not to say that Welsh rugby was not without its own problems. When the valley clubs were involved matches could also resemble dour internecine warfare. But that went on largely unnoticed by the English press. Meanwhile, the premier Welsh clubs were roving far and wide around England, taking the chance to further enhance their on-field reputations for open exciting play against less well organised opponents and drawing good crowds into the bargain.

Under remorseless pressure from Association Football at home, the northern clubs had laid themselves open to a charge that they had become too insular and too mired in a political battle of wills to alter their style of play. That failure to address the bigger picture would haunt the northern clubs when, after a year of mounting tension and ill-will, the split in the RFU over 'broken-time' and the restructuring of senior club competitive rugby finally came to a head as the close season drew to an end.

Seriously concerned about the RFU's intentions, 22 clubs voted to resign and form the Northern Union (NU) on Thursday 29 August 1895. There were high hopes for the rebels' future success. In an interview with the *Bradford Daily Argus* on 31 August, Fred Cooper, the Bradford winger and captain of the club for the previous season, caught the mood when he said he believed the NU "was likely to improve the game and increase spectator interest". Such high expectations were embraced by the new union. Those improvements would, however, prove to pose a more daunting challenge than any of the founders could have imagined.

First, however, the new season's fixtures had to be restructured. In response to the northern clubs' secession the RFU ruled five days later that no fixtures between its clubs and the rebels would be permissible. Within a couple of weeks, the RFU's stance had been supported by the other three home unions. Contrary to what might have been expected there was no general outcry at the RFU AGM held in London on 19 September and no semblance of a concerted campaign to maintain contact at least in the short-term. With less than three weeks to go before the new season would be getting underway, the split threw English rugby's fixtures into disarray. Oldham had been expecting to open the new RFU season with a much anticipated prestige visit from Swansea on Saturday 21 September. As things turned out, the formation of the NU meant that Oldham's season began two weeks earlier and the match against Swansea had to be cancelled, as did the return in south Wales at Christmas. The rebel breakaway had immediately called time on one longstanding rivalry that had been part of a highly competitive decade long relationship between the clubs of northern England and south Wales.

Only a couple of leading northern clubs were in a position to maintain contact. One of them, Swinton, seemed determined for a while to single-handedly uphold northern prestige. As winter loomed Swinton enjoyed a comfortable home victory over Swansea, then managed to hold the 'All Whites' to a draw at St Helen's during the festive period.

Early in the New Year, Swinton came out on top after a hard-fought encounter with Cardiff at Chorley Road. Three months later, with their club's future allegiance under serious discussion, Swinton's players travelled south once more to fulfil the return fixture with Cardiff. The 'Lions' were dire at the Arms Park on 6 April 1896, conceding six tries in a 26–0 defeat. The local paper, the *Swinton and Pendlebury Journal*, lamented that "The wretched exhibition with which the Blues are closing the season is unaccountable".

Was it unaccountable? It is easy to believe that with a critical choice on the club's future looming the players would be taking sides and that would hardly have made for a cohesive effort. Whatever the reason it marred what would be their last ever meeting. It was sad that meetings between the leading northern and Welsh clubs, whose clash of styles had often been one of the main highlights of the season, should effectively end on such a low note.

Massive disruption of teams and fixtures in England's northern counties was only to be expected after the exit of the rebel group. It might have been expected to affect the national team, but initially that did not seem to be the case. Missing many of the likely choices who had followed their clubs into the NU, the North's selectors drew upon the region's strength in depth to meet the nation's need. Having recorded a surprising win, 11–3, over the South at Hartlepool on 14 December, an experimental North XV supplied 10 players – five backs and five uncapped forwards – to an England XV that met Wales at Blackheath three weeks later. Led by the Northumbrian half-back, Rockliff's Billy Taylor, the forward based northern game-plan still appeared to be too strong. Depleted by injury the visitors were overpowered, conceding seven tries, in a 25–0 defeat. It was the third successive victory for England and one that seemed however briefly to suggest that English rugby had not been seriously weakened.

In south Wales the split in English rugby seemed to have little initial resonance, local supporters remaining confident that they were watching rugby of the highest quality. 'Welsh Athlete', writing in the *Western Mail* of Monday 25 November 1895 after over 20,000 had watched the second meeting of the season between Cardiff and Newport stated that "Whatever may be the interest attached to international or county games, so far as Cardiff and Newport are concerned it pales before the fierce fire of enthusiasm that burns on the occasion of matches between the two towns, who have come to be looked upon as the leading exponents of the Rugby code probably throughout the United Kingdom ... the games have always proved open, scientific, and interesting tactics, and it is this, and this alone, that has resulted in their engagements being so consistently maintained".

Blinded by the strength of Welsh confidence, it seemed to many people in the press that there was no need to look elsewhere for the best. Following Llanelli's decisive victory at Newport on Saturday 27 February 1897, which maintained the club's season-long unbeaten run, a reporter for the *Daily Chronicle*, a national daily published in London, could proclaim "The club championship of the United Kingdom may unhesitatingly be awarded to the Llanelli fifteen." Unhesitatingly? There had only been an 18-month separation at that point but for that awestruck reporter it appeared that the NU's leading clubs had completely ceased to be worthy of his consideration.

Over the same year-and-a-half the northern rebels had set about putting flesh on the bare bones of their new union. Having taken control of their own destiny, there were some within the NU who dared to dream of a different game, one at odds with the prevailing northern style. This radical school of thought wanted a rethink on scrummaging and team size. Just six days after the NU's first season had opened, Halifax took the lead and proposed that the NU should reduce teams to 13-a-side.

Harry Sewell, a member of the Leeds committee, expressed his support for this proposal to a reporter from the *Yorkshire Post*.

According to Sewell, the NU had to make the game as open as possible as this was the key to future success. Sewell's views were summed up by the *Post* reporter as follows: "scrummaging is not an attractive portion of the game and the reduction of the number of forwards will, it is considered, give the backs a better chance of playing a fast open game". Although that proposal was unsuccessful, Halifax did not give up and sent a team to Manningham to take part in a trial match, played 13-a-side (using a round ball) with no line-outs, on Tuesday 1 October 1895. While the trial found favour with some of the spectators present, the players had strong reservations, fearing that the game would become faster than they could stand. Despite those reservations it was an idea whose time had not yet come.

Two weeks later, at its first committee meeting on 17 October, such radicalism was put to one side. The committee concentrated on clarifying the NU's stance on what were seen as the crucial questions. Professionalism was probably top of the list. Refuting the view of the RFU, it was declared illegal. To ensure there was no misunderstanding a professional was defined as someone who received any money consideration whatever for services to his club above bona fide loss of earnings. Payment for players who missed work, or 'broken-time' payments as they were better known, was set at a maximum of 6/- (£0.30) per day with the rider that only one day's payment could be claimed for each match. No other payments, such as expenses for training would be permitted.

As the rebels' first season drew to a close, anyone who harboured hopes of reconciliation between the NU and the RFU had to recognise that there was no realistic possibility of that happening. Even the very real threat of losing more clubs to the NU – and the rumours that were circulating set that figure high – were not enough to get the RFU to change its stance. RFU intransigence meant it was inevitable that season by season, the north's strength in depth would defect to the rebels. To accommodate them the NU was going to have to chart its own independent course. At a committee meeting on 5 March 1896 a discussion took place on the NU's long-term plans and it was decided to set up county based league competitions and to offer a challenge cup for competition the following season.

Open to all its member clubs, the NU Challenge Cup was English rugby's first open club competition and as it provided inter-county fixtures it rapidly assumed the role of the game's most prestigious competition. Its final rapidly became the most important date on the NU's calendar.

It would be just over a year before the rebel union's major club competition got underway. To add stature to the competition the NU committee commissioned a handsome silver trophy at a cost of £50.

From an initial entry of 52 clubs Batley and St Helens emerged to contest the first Final at Headingley, the NU's most prestigious ground, on Saturday 24 April 1897. Any visitor from afar would not have found too much shockingly new that day. As well as being played under RFU laws, the finalists' pre-match preparation, controlled by the NU's slightly liberalised amateurism, meant that the fitness levels and game-plans would have been little different from those seen at big matches pre-split. Batley's 'Gallant Youths' lived up to their billing as favourites, winning 10–3 to become the first recipients of the new trophy and be lauded as the champions of the North.

Although the final had only drawn a rather disappointing crowd of 13,492, paying £624, the *Leeds Mercury* described the event as "An auspicious beginning" and went on to say that it was "'A big success, financially, socially and from a football point of view". There was a much less sympathetic assessment in the extensive reporting of the *Yorkshire Post*. Faint praise for the match and doubts about the long-term success of the venture was the flavour of the report in that paper. "The match itself was fast and well contested and up to the average standard of local Cup-ties in the character of football shown. No one thinks of looking to a cup-tie for the highest forms of football skill. Endurance, pluck and safe tactics are usually the qualities that command success. Saturday's game compared favourably with the majority of its predecessors."

Batley won through to the final again the following year. Once again, they showed the strength of their defence, conceding just a single try over the six rounds of the competition. This time Bradford provided the opposition at Headingley. Having a big city club contest for the final helped greatly in swelling the crowd to 27,941, with receipts of £1,586, which was claimed to be a record for any match held under the auspices of either the NU or the RFU.

After a low scoring match, the trophy stayed in Batley largely because once again its pack got the better of the opposition's eight and controlled the play. Although there had been little free-flowing play, the match was still considered to have been "very fast and open for a final tie". A rising attendance gave good grounds for hope that the new competition was starting to be embraced by the game's supporters. It needed to, for the NU, struggling to consolidate its own identity, was pinning its hopes on the Challenge Cup having what was needed to become its flagship club competition and raise its profile both north and south of the River Trent. To do that it would be even better if its final would showcase all that was best about the rebel game as well.

As the NU cautiously hoped for the future success of its Challenge Cup competition, the Welsh XV, as near to a glamour side as possible at the time, continued to capture the British public's imagination through the pages of the sporting press. Through those pages Arthur Gould had had become rugby's best known player. That fame proved to be Gould's undoing and he was forced to withdraw from the international arena with a record number of caps to his name, following his acceptance of a substantial testimonial raised by his many admirers.

The style of play Gould had championed lived on and prospered as the Welsh selectors proved adept at both building from within and learning from their opponents. Under Gould's successor, Swansea's Billy Bancroft, the Welsh national team ended the last International Championship of the nineteenth century on a new high.

Time had caught up with many of Gould's team and the selectors were forced to bring in seven debutants for the visit of England. News broke that to make Bancroft's job easier, the much changed team was to be brought together for a full day's preparation on the Thursday before of the match. One of the paradoxes of the situation was that members of the amateur Welsh team could take time off from their jobs, unpaid of course, to practice – an act that would have contravened the professional NU's work clauses.

As far as the Welsh Football Union (WFU) was concerned it was time and money well spent. Having got the upper-hand up front, the Welsh backs were able to turn on the style, their wingers running in six tries. By the end the Welsh had inflicted the heaviest defeat to date on a hapless, enfeebled England with a 26–3 win. With all matches in the Principality off, there was an attendance of 25,000, paying £1,500, just short of the NU held British record.

As had become the norm, the local press heaped praise on the Welsh performance. 'Welsh Athlete' writing in the *Western Mail* on the following Monday, 9 January 1899, confidently asserted that Wales had "proved conclusively on Saturday that, not only in club football, but in representative matches, our football is stronger, more scientific, and of a better class all round than that of the amateur organisations now owing allegiance to the English Rugby Union".

He went on to state that "The Northern Union need not enter particularly into our calculations, except so far as to suggest that England's strength undoubtedly lies in their ranks." It appeared the NU could be placed outside those calculations and would remain there until its clubs had worked out a way to more effectively use that undoubted strength.

'Old Ebor', who had travelled to Swansea for the match, reflected on the WFU's team-strengthening efforts on his way home. Writing in the *Yorkshire Evening Post* on Wednesday 11 January he was loath to condemn a day he felt was the product of keenness on Wales' part. However, he related that it had been put to him "that the proceeding suggests a serious, business like spirit not quite in keeping with the traditions of amateur football" and he could understand concerns about this. That business like approach would continue although the WFU would be more circumspect in future about practice days. The team's style on the field would not be affected. Articles describing the Welsh as playing as keenly and earnestly as professionals would appear regularly in English, Irish and Scottish newspapers over the next half-dozen years.

In response the WFU would issue denials and denounce accusations of professionalism, but they would not be allowed to stifle the team's ambition or invention. Time and effort invested in developing further specialisation at half-back and among the forwards would soon pay dividends, enabling the men in red to stay ahead of their rivals and begin a decade-long run of success that would in time be dubbed Welsh rugby's 'Golden Era'.

From the sports pages it would have appeared that the most attractive 'professional' approach in rugby was to be found in the ranks of the 'old', Welsh, game.

With the internationals drawing ever larger crowds and gate receipts, rugby in the Principality was awash with unbounded self-confidence and continued to be publicly disdainful of anything being attempted by the professionals in the north of England. The thought must have crossed the minds of many involved with the NU – would Association Football be exerting such pressure if its clubs were playing with a Welsh style that was capable of generating such a high level of self-confidence? But nagging doubts remained. Could Welsh style be sustained under the work clauses and could it cope with the demands of a hotly contested northern league competition?

That course of action was always a possibility for the NU's leading clubs. By the turn of the century the NU's clubs had recruited large numbers of Welsh players, a few of them with Welsh international caps to their name. Much might have been expected from a couple of those capped players who had led premier Welsh clubs but, in the end, neither Owen Badger (Llanelli) nor Viv Huzzey (Cardiff) were able to settle at their new clubs, Swinton and Oldham respectively, and therefore never got the chance to apply their captaincy skills.

In the days before club coach-managers came on the scene, responsibility for the team was split, the committee taking charge of selection and recruitment while the captain looked after performance. Operating as a sort of early player-coach, the captain's job was to draw on his experience to organise and focus his players to the team's best tactical advantage. Welsh team formation had been the norm at every NU club for a few years, but none appear to have seriously contemplated playing with more of a Welsh style. There was a chance that that might change when a couple of uncapped Welshmen with somewhat lesser profiles than Badger and Huzzey accepted the challenge of captaincy at two leading clubs. Their appointment raised the possibility that their teams might challenge the northern orthodoxy and employ a more scientific style.

The first was Tom Williams who had been on Salford's roster for less than 12 months when he was handed the leadership of a largely Welsh squad in August 1898. He held the position for the next four years during which time the 'Reds' settled into a forward-dominated style and earned a reputation more for roughness than science.

Although they came close to honours, the 'Reds' could not achieve a victory in either the 1900 or 1902 NU Cup Finals. When, in summer 1903, Huddersfield's committee had to find a new captain, they shifted their focus and appointed Tom Williams' fellow countryman and threequarter, Llewellyn Deere. With three years' experience of the northern game behind him, Deere was given the job of reviving the fortunes of a team, with a sizeable Welsh contingent that was finding life tough in the NRL.

Hopes of an upturn in fortune soon foundered and by the end of a very disappointing season Huddersfield had suffered the indignity of relegation to the Second Division. The team did not gel and it was the captain who bore the brunt of the criticism. Just a few days after the final heavy defeat, the writer of the 'Football Chat' column in the *Huddersfield Daily Examiner* mounted a scathing attack on Deere. For him Deere's selection as captain "was responsible to a great extent for the gradual decay into (the) hopeless incompetence shown by our team."

Williams and Deere were not novices, both having enjoyed successful spells of captaincy in the highly competitive valley-centred Glamorgan League before moving north, but in the closely fought higher echelons of the NU something was missing. Perhaps that was because having signed for a NU club, the majority of the Welsh players who made the transition successfully, and there were many, could only maintain aspects of their national style on an individual basis. One such player was 'Wattie' Davies who left Cardiff for Batley as a young uncapped winger in October 1896. For the next decade Davies regularly finished on top of his new club's try scoring list. Welsh flair would manifest itself in his brilliant unorthodox play but it had very little influence on the play of what was an archetypal Yorkshire team.

The stadium at Fallowfield, the venue for the 1899 NU Cup Final, had its drawbacks, being neither convenient nor well appointed, factors which in a city being colonised by Association Football contributed to an attendance below expectations. Venues for future finals were the prerogative of the NU committee and the correspondent of the *Yorkshire Post* was led by some sections of its membership to write in his report of the match for Monday's edition that the NU might "even try the experiment of taking it to the Crystal Palace. Such a course would be a bold tackling of the Rugby Union in their own stronghold."

Since opening four years earlier, the vast stadium at Crystal Palace in south London had become the nation's premier football venue, the setting for the FA Cup final where annually the possibilities unleashed by the wholehearted embrace of professionalism were put on display.

A year later, Swinton, whose team was rated by many as playing the best football through the rounds of the Cup, had qualified to meet their near neighbours Salford, once again at Fallowfield. In his report of that final, held on Saturday 28 April 1900, the correspondent of the *Yorkshire Post*, was enthused to write that "From the commencement the play delighted everybody, the backs on both sides handling the ball beautifully, and indulging in many brilliant bits of passing that might with advantage by emulated by the 'punt and rush' artists of Yorkshire."

Dismay at the punt and rush style, employed widely in Yorkshire, had featured in many of his reports over the season. Swinton's outstanding display saw them claim victory 18–8 to take the trophy back to Lancashire for the first time.

As the nineteenth century passed into history, the NU's membership was now much larger than the Rugby Union's in the north of England. That membership shrinkage meant that no trace of the old rugby game was to be found in large parts of Cumberland, Lancashire and Yorkshire. While it might have assumed control of the rugby game in large parts of the north the mood of the rebel body was hardly celebratory. Despite the success of the latest final, it was clear that the NU had mounting problems, brought on by a growing self-doubt. In such circumstances it was hard to imagine the rebel leadership making any bold move like a switch to Crystal Palace. Professionalism legalised in June 1898 under strict regulations, the so-called work clauses which required regular outside employment, had made it even easier for players to be recruited from far and wide.

In terms of raw talent, the NU's leading teams were stronger than ever, provided they could avoid the punishments handed out for contravening the professional regulations. Those regulations made it mandatory for players to work all their contracted hours each week even if that required them to attend their place of work on Saturday mornings. Onerous day jobs, however, appeared to be doing little to help meet the rising expectations of professionalism. Was this the way to a better game?

The growing pains of professional rugby had been making the news all that season. The weekly magazine *Yorkshire Chat* had given over its letters page for a debate on the merits of the rival football games in autumn 1899. There was a letter from Hull's long-serving threequarter and former captain, Charles Lempriere, in the issue for 7 October. Lempriere, who played as an amateur, praised full professionalism for raising Association Football to a level far ahead of rugby. He then went on to state optimistically that "Rugby has recently followed suit. In four years, she [the NU] has made rapid strides; she is becoming 'scientific' and 'skilful' too. Soon she will be on level terms in this respect once more". It was a rousing prospect that Lempriere offered and one that he believed would lead to greater support. Lempriere's playing career would draw to a close soon afterwards and so too it appeared would his hopes for the benefits of professionalism to show results.

It was the ill effects of professionalism that were more immediately being felt. They left some leading figures in Yorkshire very unhappy and a few began to air their grave doubts about professionalism and its impact on the field of play in public. It could be seen most clearly in the discussions at Manningham, the rebel's inaugural league champions.

Ejected from the NU Cup in the first round and having finished a poor ninth in the YSC, there was no doubt 1899–00 had been a disappointing season. Although the club's gates had held up well, the quality of football on display had not pleased all involved. Along with financial issues, dissatisfaction surfaced at the club's AGM. The *Yorkshire Post,* on 24 May 1900, reported the club's outgoing President, James Freeman, expressing his wish that "they must go back, if possible, to that free and independent style of amateur play". This was obviously not just a lone view as Antonio Fattorini, a member of the club committee and a leading figure in the NU, was reported as also saying that he "thought it would be best for the cause if they could get back to the free and independent amateur style of play".

Manningham's leaders were not alone in being underwhelmed by the NU's style of play, which was leading to the attacking game being smothered by a tighter, more defensively minded, style of play. At the NU AGM held seven weeks after Manningham's, on 17 July, Joe Nicholl (Halifax), the honorary treasurer, stressed the importance of the task facing the legislators saying "Our action this day means either the fall of the Northern Union or its continuance. Our clubs do not stand in a good position financially ... There is another game – Association – that is making headway, and they are doing so because they play a more attractive game. At present we have the forwards working like Trojans while the backs are standing unable to get the ball."

In response, the incoming President of the NU, Herbert Hutchinson (Wakefield Trinity), drew the attention of those present to a match 10 weeks earlier commenting that "if Salford and Swinton could play such a game as they did in the Cup Final ... and others could not there must be something wrong with the players and not with the game." If it was a player issue then better preparation might well have been the answer.

Hutchinson, however, was certainly not an advocate of anything close to full professionalism.

With few believing more of the same was an option, something had to be done if northern rugby was going to regain its ability to win stylishly within the laws of the game. Two distinct courses of action were advanced – law changes and open professionalism. The dilemma of which of those to prioritise has been with the game ever since. At the time it was the former that was pursued most avidly. Changes were made to a number of the laws. Changes clearing up anomalies or undue restrictions that were highlighted by competitive fixtures, such as to the knock-on law, were well received.

Other changes, most obviously the ones to the tackle law and the return of the ball into play from touch, proved more contentious. Unintentionally, the latter changes generally left the game even more dominated by the scrummage than before. It was not the hoped for outcome and obviously did not lead to any noticeable improvement in the quality of play.

Those doubts would prove persistent. At Headingley at the end of April 1901, the Cup Final brought together two clubs that had enjoyed reasonably successful seasons – Batley, fourth in the Yorkshire Senior Competition, and Warrington, sixth in its Lancashire equivalent (LSC). The meeting of those two clubs was eagerly anticipated and the match attracted a new record crowd of 29,569, with receipts of £1,645. Batley went on to record a remarkable third success in the five years the Cup had been running through two first-half tries, 6–0.

Unfortunately, the meeting of two very defensively proficient teams was not universally appreciated. The correspondent of the *Bradford Observer* was decidedly underwhelmed, his report saying that "very few of the 30,000 spectators ... could have been anything but dissatisfied with the match as an exhibition of scientific football. In the main the play was of a scrambling, rough-and-tumble character, unrelieved by no more than half-a-dozen bits of really smart work ... The first half was passable in regard to the sport, but the second period dragged fearfully, roughness alone giving place to monotony."

It appeared that the rebel game's showcase event seemed destined to alternate between good years and bad. Sadly, the bad years seemed to coincide with the highest attendances.

Just three years after it had hoped that the level of professionalism within the game had been settled, voices calling for a radical overhaul of the rebel body looked certain to force the NU to open a new debate on the game's future direction. With the regular season all but over, those voices were brought together at a private, informal meeting, organised by Halifax on Wednesday 17 April 1901. There, the top six clubs from each of the Senior Competitions aired their disenchantment with the current state of the game. There was general dissatisfaction at the quality of some of the intra-county matches they were compelled to play, the poor, not to say rough style of play adopted by some of the teams, and the unattractiveness of some of the engagements.

By comparison, some of the inter-county ties in the NU Cup had produced good football and attracted better crowds than even top of the table league matches. It was considered that if the top clubs combined in a new league the result would be a series of matches that would command the support of the public by reason of the superior quality of the football.

After much negotiation, a plan for a new league was put to the NU committee on 6 June. Thanks to the co-option of two more founder members, the seventh placed clubs on either side of the Pennines, into the new league the vote was carried on the NU committee by 12 votes to 11. That vote meant there would be a Northern Rugby League (NRL) for season 1901–02. The price of that victory however, was the shelving of many League members' hopes of a move to a more unrestricted professionalism and the rejection of any immediate move to bring in new members from outside the NU.

The launch of the NRL briefly seemed set to end some of the pessimism that was shrouding the NU. Much of that was down to Broughton Rangers who dominated the inaugural season. Led by their inspirational centre, Bob Wilson, the Rangers showed a new found attacking force, marrying a northern pack with a creative back division drawn from across Britain. Losing only four of their 26 matches the Rangers had the NRL title wrapped up by February and finished 12 points clear of the runner-up, Salford. The Rangers, the League's top scorers, also had a chance of completing the double at the first attempt when they faced near neighbours Salford in the NU Cup Final at Rochdale's Athletic Grounds on Saturday 26 April. On the big day the Rangers overwhelmed the 'Reds' by five tries and five goals – 25–0.

Some of the Rangers' joy was tempered by a run-in with the professional regulations. Word reached the NU committee that a number of the Rangers' players had missed work on the morning of the final. They had and for that the club had to be punished, even if it was the biggest day on the game's calendar. For breaching the work clauses, the Rangers were fined £10 a couple of weeks later.

The Rangers' performance was widely acclaimed. Having been underwhelmed 12 months earlier the reporter from the *Bradford Observer* this time was greatly impressed. After quoting fellow spectators who had described the match as "A glorious climax to a brilliant season" and "The most wonderful final on record" he went on to add that it was a match that "in years to come will be referred to as one of the greatest games in the annals of Northern Unionism".

An early picture of Harold Wagstaff. (Courtesy Robert Gate)

Sadly, the Rangers' glory days proved short-lived, their team falling away from those high levels of attacking prowess quite rapidly. They proved unable to defend either of their honours the following season, finishing fifth in the NRL and going out of the NU Cup in the first round. As the Rangers' strength ebbed, clubs that favoured the old northern style stepped up to reclaim centre stage.

As the clubs readied themselves for the start of the NU Cup competition, they did so against a backdrop of mounting disquiet. An article in the *Bradford Daily Telegraph* for Wednesday 14 January 1903 went so far as to talk of an impending crisis for the NU. At its heart was the failure of the NU and NRL to meet the demand for 'good football' and this was leading to a declining interest in the rugby game. To meet that demand football enthusiasts were said to be meeting privately to plan the formation of professional soccer clubs.

In a letter published two days later, 'Soccer' wrote that in his opinion "local sportsmen were simply tired of Rugby football, with its wearisome iteration of scrummages and dull play." Much of that dull play resulted from the tight defences that were taking over and were threatening to throttle the life out of the game.

A few clubs had become adept at this negative approach but one in particular exploited this strategy much better than all the rest. Over that season, Halifax set new standards for defensive play and it enabled them to emulate the Rangers' feat and complete the double of League and Cup. Over the club's 42 league and cup matches only 95 points would be conceded and its line would only be crossed on 19 occasions. In fact, Halifax managed to restrict the opposition scoring tries to just 13 matches and nilled its opponents on no less than 21 occasions. Other First Division clubs deserve a mention for playing dour defence-bound football. Over the 37 matches – 34 league and three cup – played that season, Leigh did not score a try in 22 of them. They scored a mere 143 points in those 37 matches. Although Leigh went out in the second round of the Cup, they did finish a creditable 12th in the top flight. Near neighbours Wigan finished four places below Leigh. At their new Central Park ground, Wigan's play could hardly have been described as spectacular – they scored just 14 tries in the 18 matches – 17 league and one cup – played there.

News of the previous season's exciting clash had helped draw spectators from all parts of the north of England for 1903's Cup Final. Headingley played host to a new record crowd of 32,507, paying £1,834, showing once again the region's continuing appetite for the rugby game. Halifax's captain for the latter half of the season was the club's veteran star half-back, Archer Rigg. Ten years earlier Rigg had been a member of Halifax's Yorkshire Rugby Union Cup winning team, the one mentioned above that had been proud to be dubbed the 'Newport of the North' for its stylish attacking play.

Salford had again reached the final and again finished on the losing side but there the similarities with the previous year's final ended. Monday's papers all agreed it was a poor game. The *Yorkshire Evening Post* report was damning saying "it is doubtful if any final tie, disappointing as final ties often are, ever produced such a poor display of scientific football." This sad display was blamed on the forwards for their crude scrummaging and gamesmanship, which took up so much of the match and worked in the end to Halifax's advantage.

Having lost a thoroughly disillusioned and financially ailing Manningham to the Football League, proposals to change some of the laws were put before the NU's members at the AGM on 18 July 1903. Addressing the issue of change very candidly, JH Smith (Widnes), a former President of the NU, told those present: "I am perfectly satisfied that unless we can give the public a higher standard of football than we saw last season, the game will not want killing, it will die a natural death." He went on to add that the forwards had become scrummaging machines and that defences were so well organised that it "was almost impossible to breakthrough".

Speaking further in support of a committee recommendation for 12-a-side teams at that meeting, Smith referred to the recent, far from interesting, Cup Final, saying of the outcome that it "gave the slightest satisfaction to nobody outside of Halifax". Regrettably the contest between the best team in Lancashire (Salford) and the best in Yorkshire (Halifax) had once again been poor. In Smith's opinion the change to 12-a-side "would afford the opportunity for individual cleverness to be exercised, without putting any restrictions on open play, do away with many undesirable scrimmages, would improve forward play and do more to revive the dribble, and make it a more prominent feature of the game than it was." The vote of 54–24 in favour was five votes short of the threequarter majority necessary to make the change. Recognising the level of support, it was agreed to test out 12-a-side in representative and junior matches in 1903–04.

Without any major changes to the NU's laws, senior club football continued to be dominated by robust defences and the best ones, like Halifax's, were almost impenetrable. With 15-a-side teams still in place, Halifax were less successful in 1903–04, but would still manage to reach the Cup Final. JH Smith was appointed as referee and got to see at first-hand how what was described as a dull match played out. Johnny Morley, the Halifax half-back and captain, took control and rarely let the ball out to his backs. It was reported that Halifax won 8–3 "largely by the method in which the forwards broke up the scrums, wheeled the ball on the Warrington backs, and thereby smashed up the latter's scoring combinations."

Winning was obviously paramount, but the professionals seemed willing to take such single-mindedness to the extreme. Contrary to the NRL's stated intentions northern professionalism was continuing to build on its reputation for dour defensive play while its attacks were being derided for their reliance on 'kick and rush' tactics or else close dribbling rushes.

In sharp contrast, thanks largely to the sporting press, rugby union was firmly identified with the attacking and entertaining play that was the hallmark of the performances of the Welsh national team and their premier clubs. The northern style was not seen as sufficiently enterprising or attractive to deter the Football League challenge or tempt the leading clubs in the English west and the midlands away from the RFU and their highly prized Welsh fixtures.

There were clear signs that arguments in favour of open professionalism as a way forward were returning to the fore when the *Athletic News* published a news item on the future of the regulations covering professionals needing to have outside employment on Monday 5 December 1904.

Written by 'Old Ebor', it updated the readers on the likelihood of another challenge to the work clauses and explained the basis of the thinking behind those working to remove them. 'Old Ebor' put forward the opposition argument that "it is idle to expect the Northern Union game to successfully compete with the Association when the players in one game are kept with their noses to the grindstone while in the other, they have nothing to do except keep in training and perfect themselves in the game which they are paid for expounding. There is considerable force in this argument too. The best of Northern Union football has not yet been seen and when one comes to think of it the players can be excused if they fall short of the ideal in their play when they are required to work hard throughout the week and allowed little time for rest and training".

Open professionalism, something that had originally been beyond the pale for the majority of the rebel clubs was now being seen as a necessity if the game was to prosper.

This realisation was occurring only a few months before the 10th anniversary of the game's split. Sadly, the main legacy of the first decade of the split seemed to have been the weakening of northern rugby. Much of its former strength was passing to the Association game which had capitalised on rugby's disarray, building a significant presence across the region, particularly in the cities. Under severe pressure the NU continued to strive for a more attractive game that could halt or even reverse rugby's decline in the region. In *The Book of Football,* JH Smith sounded almost worn down by the unequal struggle with the RFU and the FA when he wrote that "no success of the English Union or development of the Association game is ever allowed to pass without the fact being advanced as indicating Northern Union decay". Despite the setbacks, Smith still retained his belief that the NU would find the ways and means to move forward. For a while longer, however, the outlook would appear even tougher.

None of the representatives who assembled at the NU's AGM on 13 June 1905 would have needed reminding of just how tough the times were. Association Football's assault was causing severe financial problems. Some professional clubs were warning they may have to close down, while others were disbanding their reserve teams to cut costs. Choosing to stay positive, a majority at the meeting voted to complete the long drawn out transition away from amateurism and legalise open professionalism. Team preparation and selection would no longer be significantly influenced by concerns about the players' employment situations. The full benefits of professionalism could now be brought to bear, but that would clearly not bring overnight improvement to the playing standards on the pitch. For those clubs with the money to back their ambitions, there was a chance to take the game forward.

Besides the possibility of an improvement in the professional ranks, it appeared that 1905–06 would be a season that served up more of the same rugby fare that had been on offer for a decade. Those expectations were to be rudely shattered by the arrival of an unheralded party of New Zealanders who disembarked at Plymouth on Friday 8 September. Two months later that party, known everywhere as the All Blacks, had taken British rugby by storm. By then, tourist victory after tourist victory had ruthlessly exposed the weaknesses of amateur rugby; the All Blacks having won their first 14 matches in England, in the process scoring 461 points while conceding just 15. Instead of being compared unfavourably with the Welsh, the NU now found itself being measured unfavourably against the All Blacks.

On Saturday 4 November the All Blacks were playing their 15th tour match, this time against England's 'premier' club, Blackheath. Even with their supposedly strongest team on the pitch, half of them internationals, Blackheath conceded seven tries as the tourists recorded their 15th victory, 32–0. 'Old Athlete' of the *Athletic News* was quoted in the *New Zealand Times* as saying he had never in 25 years' experience seen so grand a display of football as that given by the New Zealanders that day. That same afternoon 200 miles to the north, Yorkshire met Lancashire at Hull in a NU County Championship match. A typically close fought Roses clash saw the visitors victorious, 8–0, thanks to a try in each half. The match report in the *Manchester Guardian* while paying a compliment to the victors undermined the standard of play, stating that although it was achieved thanks "to a clever back division and a better conception of the possibilities of Rugby football", it did so before adding that it was done "without approaching the standard to which the New Zealanders have attained in passing and running, (although) the Lancastrians gave a really good exhibition in these arts."

This disappointing assessment was published when there was still another month before NU supporters in any significant numbers would get the chance to see for themselves how good the All Blacks actually were. With 25 consecutive victories behind them, the All Blacks travelled north to take on Cheshire at Birkenhead Park on Saturday 9 December. As expected, the tourists easily disposed of a Cheshire side weakened by injuries and other commitments, running in 10 tries in a 34–0 victory, in front of a capacity crowd of 8,000. According to press reports, the quality of the All Blacks' display came as something of a surprise to the NU supporters in the crowd. Summing up the All Blacks' display the correspondent of the *Liverpool Courier* commented that "it is their deadly machine-like combination and tactful skill which make them so absolutely pre-eminent".

Four days later, trade in Leeds was said to be paralysed as a huge crowd of 23,683, paying £1,150, assembled at Headingley. Despite the inevitable signs of staleness among the touring party, those present could only watch in awe as the All Blacks once again scored 10 tries to overwhelm an outclassed Yorkshire XV 40–0 to extend their unbeaten run to 27 matches. In his report, the *Yorkshire Post* correspondent commented that "Generally speaking, one was forced to the conviction that the New Zealanders played football in a way which we had not seen before" and "the only difference between one engagement and the other is that new resource and further possibilities of football appear to be developed from match to match … no such combination of speed and ambi-dexterousness has ever been seen in this country". Despite the one-sided nature of the match 'Old Ebor' still felt able in his 'Notes on the Game' in the *Yorkshire Evening Post* to label it "the biggest Rugby match of modern times".

So much praise annoyed many in the north. One of them was Fred Cooper, the Welsh wing who had joined Bradford over a decade earlier. Interviewed by the *Daily Mail* Cooper sounded exasperated as well he might as he gave his assessment of the Yorkshire match. "The wearers of the silver fern have not been defeated, but they have not played the cream of English football. Such men play under the banner of the Northern Union. The men who opposed New Zealand at Headingley are the weakest lot who ever donned Yorkshire jerseys, and the visitors did not achieve anything out of the common when they beat them". The only way to test Fred Cooper's assertion was if a representative NU XV could take on the All Blacks. According to at least one member of the touring party, a marginalised NU tried to capitalise on press speculation by making an offer, backed by a good guarantee, to the All Blacks' management for an end of tour charity match but nothing could come of it.

Having failed to get a stage on which the professionals could prove their mettle, the NU could only watch in envy as a highly motivated and well prepared Welsh XV rose to the occasion at Cardiff Arms Park on Saturday 16 December. In the run-up to the match, the WFU invested a lot of time and effort into preparing its team. The sides were so evenly matched that the game became a hard fought, occasionally rough, scrambling encounter. It was a solitary pre-planned first-half try, the result of an unorthodox Welsh move, that divided the two teams at the final whistle.

What did the watching journalists make of the match? For 'Forward' of the *Western Mail* the victory, and in particular that winning score, was not down to all that pre-match preparation, but was "creditable to the genius of Welsh football." That such a close fought encounter could enthral the vast crowd was, according to the match report in Monday's *South Wales Daily News*, due to the open character of the play: "Seldom was the ball hidden from sight for more than a moment."

Not every pressman agreed. The representative of the *Yorkshire Post* was not overly impressed by the quality of the play commenting that "Great though the match was, it is impossible to describe it as an exhibition of high-class football. On the contrary, so far from being an exposition of the styles of play that have made the reputation of each one of the combatants stand so high in the football world, it was rather one great strenuous cup-tie". This was not the first time that Welsh style had been stifled by a well organised defence, but on this day, it was considered an unimportant factor by most of those present.

What impressed all the press corps was how an international match had grown into rugby's first truly great occasion. Ignoring the lack of points, 'Forward' could still heap praise on the occasion saying: "Other victories have been won in other years, and while they served to establish the supremacy of Welsh football in these islands, they pale into dimness in comparison with the great triumph of Saturday. Such a game had never been played before, and such a victory had never been won." Swollen by excursionists drawn from across England, the gate receipts, £2,650, were a new British rugby record. This was rugby elevated to a new level. As 'Forward' said of the match "It was virtually a contest for the Rugby championship of the world".

It was a development of huge significance and one that was then far beyond the NU's conception. The tour had proved a massive success and one that British Rugby Union looked set to exploit further with the first South African party due to arrive in the coming September.

After such an epic encounter, newspaper interest in Fred Cooper's earlier assertion passed and his rating of the NU's strength would remain an unproven footnote. Only a minority of the best known journalists even in the north of England subscribed to Cooper's estimation. The majority of journalists remained in thrall to the brilliance of the Welsh XV. 'Flaneur', whose bye-line appeared in the *Leeds Mercury*, was fairly typical of that group of journalists when in the aftermath of the defeat of the All Blacks he wrote for the paper's Monday edition "It is, however, appropriate that the Welsh International team should have been the first side to haul down the New Zealand flag, for Rugby football finds no keener adherents in the British Isles than in the Principality; and the Welshmen have of late years been quite the most brilliant exponents of the code."

Having met the best that British Rugby Union had to offer and suffered just a single defeat, the All Blacks departed these shores on 20 January at the start of their long journey home. There had been some easy victories, but they should not be allowed to detract from their near perfect record. The tourists were a very powerful squad containing many brilliant players, who had been expertly moulded into a well drilled combination by their captain and vice-captain. They had made a huge impression on British rugby. If that was not enough to ensure victory over the mostly scratch teams they faced in England then their athletic superiority, the result of a professional lifestyle, which required them only to play or train for rugby on a full-time basis certainly did.

What was different was that all their players passed the ball well and both forwards and backs combined in passing movements. Unlike most English packs, their forwards treated the scrum as just a way of restarting the game, their aim purely to win the ball if possible, heel it quickly out to their backs if they did, then break from the scrum and rejoin the play as soon as practicable. What was also startling was the priority they gave to possession. The ball was carried forward at pace by quick, precise passing. Kicking was largely restricted to when they were behind their own 25-yard (22 metre) line or when it was wet. It was a radical approach to rugby and it generated much appreciative comment.

Much as the authorities would have liked to prevent them, while on tour some members of the All Blacks took time out to meet with NU representatives. What happened next would change both the NU and the world of rugby forever. There was so much to admire about the visitors' play that it was inevitable that professional clubs wanted to sign them. There was undoubted interest, but there would be no immediate influx of New Zealand expertise. Rather than signing individually for English clubs at the tour's end, a group of All Blacks grouped around George Smith, their electrifying threequarter, decided they would work with the NU on a far more ambitious longer-term project. They would return home, confront a hostile Rugby Union establishment and try to raise another All Black party, one that was strong enough to mount a professional tour of Britain under the auspices of the NU.

NU hopes that the new season would end on a high note rested as usual on the Cup Final, scheduled for Saturday 28 April 1906. Once again, those hopes were to be dashed. Several showers of rain and sleet on the morning might have dampened spectator enthusiasm but even so the attendance of just 15,834, paying £920, the lowest at Headingley since 1897, was very disappointing.

Just as at the Arms Park it was a very close, intense struggle and there was only one try scored by Bradford, but there the similarity ended for the gentlemen of the press. 'Flaneur' was at Headingley as usual for the match and he was once again extremely disappointed by what he saw, saying gloomily in Monday's edition of the *Mercury* that "there was hardly a glimpse of good, open, class football".

His counterpart from the *Yorkshire Post* did not mince his words either saying that "skill in tactics was painfully lacking, and, taken as an exhibition of the handling game, the match cannot have strengthened the local hold of the Rugby pastime. Something more than fierce scrummaging and keen tackling was required and unfortunately this something was not forthcoming." The continued absence of that important something was not good news for the game or either finalist – Bradford or Salford – all three being under serious threat from Association Football interests. While the game's leadership could wait in hope for a spark of inspiration or even a touch of genius to arrive and enliven play, it was clear that something more practical had to be done – and done quickly – if the rugby game was to survive as a major force in the northern counties.

A truly remarkable season had left the NU under even greater pressure than before. It had certainly produced much food for thought and the NU's leaders were left to consider their options as summer approached. Top of the list of items to be chewed over and digested was the impact of the All Blacks' tour and the new found appetite of the British public for the Rugby Union game. This had been clear for all to see at the All Blacks' matches against England and Wales which had both drawn record crowds of well over 40,000. Clearly the laws of the RFU had not proved a block to assembling such numbers. According to JH Smith in the *Book of Football,* the NU's laws for 1905–06, after a decade of trial and error, had just three relatively minor differences from those of the RFU. And yet the laws of the NU seemed continually to be unable to deliver the same spectator appeal.

Also, if, as Fred Cooper had claimed, the cream of British rugby was playing in its ranks why was play in the NRL so dour? Seeking a way forward, the NU's members once again turned their attention to the laws of the game in a bid to improve the quality of professional play. Perhaps more by coincidence than co-ordination the NU drew a line under nearly 10 years of experimentation and made its definitive break with three key elements of the laws as framed by the RFU.

After a difficult gestation, significant changes in how the game was played were made at the AGM held on Tuesday 12 June when three unrelated resolutions created the basis for the emergence of a very different game. Essentially, this came about as the game's leadership tried to answer three main needs, to keep the ball on the field, in play and visible as much as possible, thereby providing more space and opportunity for individual skills to shine. Of those three, ball visibility was thought to be particularly important as it was considered to be a major contributor to the growing popularity of the NU's main winter rivals.

First, the meeting reconsidered reducing the number of players in a team, a proposal that had narrowly failed to be enacted three years earlier. Various proposals were presented ranging from 14 players down to 12. Despite the attention of those present being drawn to the fact that the All Blacks had produced stunning rugby with 15-a-side, from the list of options the meeting chose, by 43 votes to 18, Warrington's proposal to reduce the number of players in a team to 13 with the expectation that this would shift the emphasis of play from weight to speed and produce a more open, spectacular game.

Second, the meeting supported Bradford's proposal to change the method of returning the ball back into play after the tackle. Since the 'split' the NU's laws governing the tackle and the RFU's had diverged with the former requiring a scrummage when the ball was fairly held in the tackle. This change had inevitably produced rather a lot of scrums. Those present agreed to return to the RFU law in a bid for greater continuity of movement. When the ball was held the RFU law governing a standing tackle required the tackled player to "… at once put the ball down between himself and his opponent's goal line", after which either side could play it with their feet. In a bid to reduce accidental injuries Oldham then proposed that the tackled player, if on the ground, be prohibited from just releasing the ball and rolling away.

Instead the game would momentarily stop while the tackled player got to his feet before he would release the ball. In effect, the restart would always proceed as if it had been a standing tackle. This change it was hoped would significantly cut the number of scrums.

Third, the meeting adopted a proposal from Oldham that in future for a team to gain territory any kick to touch other than a penalty would require the ball to bounce in the field of play. If it went into touch on the full, then play would resume with a scrummage, not at the point at which the ball went into touch, but in line with the point at which it was kicked. This change not only shifted the emphasis to keeping the ball in hand but also forced teams to employ more skilful tactical kicking thereby curbing the aimless defensive punting to touch that had previously blighted so many matches.

With these changes approved the legislators ended their deliberations hoping that they had made the right choice and that taken together they would help restore the game's self-confidence.

There was no stipulation in the first law change as to how the reduction to 13 players should be achieved, Oldham's amendment to make a uniform reduction in the number of forwards to seven having been rejected. In practice nearly all clubs made plans to reduce the pack's influence on play by removing two forwards. Some clarification on the second law change concerning the tackle was called for by a number of member clubs before the season began. It was forthcoming at a meeting of the NU committee on 17 August. That meeting ruled that to reduce roughness and scrambling play a tackled player must always regain his feet before dropping the ball to the ground and bringing it back into play.

The leadership of the NU hoped they had laid the basis for a new more open form of the rugby game. One that was capable of regaining the initiative from its rivals. The verdict on what those legislators had actually achieved would not be made known until the results of their labours had been tried and tested on the pitch. Whether they were judged a success or not would depend on how the professionals would choose to interpret them. Hopefully, the vision of those professionals – young and old – would soon enable the NU's leading teams to shake off the old mindset and capitalise on the new possibilities, both on and off the pitch that had been provided. If fortune really did favour the brave then in a couple of seasons the NU game would be transformed into the exciting spectacle that had been so earnestly desired for a decade. Although it would have been hard to recognise it in those embattled times there really was a world of opportunity opening up for any talented player who thought deeply about the game. This then was the pressured world of northern rugby that was waiting to welcome young Harold Wagstaff in the autumn of 1906.

Harold Wagstaff as a young Huddersfield player.
(Courtesy Robert Gate)

Part 2: In his own words

Rugby League's Greatest Centre

The following articles were a series in the *Yorkshire Sports Post*, published weekly from 9 February 1935. Some minor editing was done to make them suitable for a book.

1. From Pump Hole to Fartown at age of 15
2. First games at Fartown
3. Rise of Huddersfield – Wrigley, Gleeson and Co.
4. Huddersfield build up a great side
5. "Scientific Obstruction" was born at Bramley
6. Finest team that ever played at Fartown
7. Memorable try that astonished Wigan
8. Our first Northern Union Cup win
9. 'Four Cups' season at Fartown
10. Men who won the four Cups
11. Some pleasant war-time contacts
12. All-star Grove Park team
13. My greatest test match

The Game I Love
Or 15 years of Northern Union Football

Excerpts from a series written by Harold Wagstaff in *All Sports Illustrated Weekly* in the spring of 1921.

The Pump Hole in Holmfirth where Harold met his young team-mates in the Pump Hole Rangers.
(Photo: Peter Lush)

Rugby League's Greatest Centre

Harold Wagstaff, captain of the Huddersfield Rugby League team at its greatest and best, and captain of the 1914 and 1920 Rugby League teams to Australia, begins in the Sports Post *this week the story of his distinguished football career.*

In it he does more than tell of personal achievement and club success-he points, all the time, to the supreme value of open football and shows to the full the influence on English football of tour teams from the Dominions.

He opens with recollections of the impression made on him, then a boy of 14, by the 1905–06 Rugby Union All Blacks. And he tells of his journey from the Pump Hole Rangers side to the Huddersfield club from which he received "five golden sovereigns" as his signing-on fee.

1. From Pump Hole to Fartown at age of 15

I am a Northern Union or Rugby League man – the name of the game has altered since first I joined it – all the way through. I was born at Underbank on 19 May 1891, and I was suckled in the Northern Union game, as it was then. You will realise this best when I tell you that I never saw a rugby union game until I witnessed the New Zealand versus New South Wales match in Australia when over there with the 1914 rugby league team.

When I lived at Underbank in the days about which I now write, the nearest rugby union club was that at Kirkstall where Headingley played. The 'split' had occurred eight or nine years earlier; and in our district, at all events, there was nothing but Northern Union football.

And it was Northern Union football all the time. My elder brother, who was my bed mate, had a local reputation as a centre threequarter with Underbank, and all the talk there was at home had to do with Rugby football. Naturally enough, I played Northern Union football – with the Pump Hole Rangers.

We took our name from the space around the village pump at Holmfirth where we held our 'committee meetings'. We had a committee room, but we never had a field of our own. Our matches, friendly affairs, were with teams of lads from the district, and there was more than one occasion on which we had to break a game in the middle to seek fresh quarters because the farmer on whose land we had set out pitch did not approve of our activities.

Big lad at 14

In those days, when I was 14 years old, I played with lads about 17 or 18, and I was bigger than most of them. We had the same aim – to get a place in the Underbank side, which then played in the Huddersfield and District League, and which afterwards had a position in the Yorkshire Senior Competition.

I was a 'flying wing-threequarter' in those far-off days, and I well remember one of the first tries I scored. We were playing Town End, from Wooldale, a village a mile or two from Underbank. The field, as I have told you, was 'borrowed', and the agreed-upon try-line – there was no question of any marking-out being done – ended near green slime, but that was something we did not discover until I, diving for my try, dived into the pond.

I remember wondering at the time whether the scoring of the try was worth the damage done to the blue and white jersey that had been bought for me by my father: one thing is certain–I did not look the smart fellow after scoring the try that I had looked when running down the field for it.

Still we were very fit in those days. We spent our spare time out of doors – we had to because there were no picture houses and no trams or buses to get us down to Huddersfield in a few minutes. If we wanted to go anywhere from Underbank, we had to walk the mile to Holmfirth station. The other way took us up over the moors into the heart of the Pennines. We were bound to be fit with all this walking.

Mad about the game

Our enthusiasm, and that of the members of the dozens of other small clubs similar to ours that were in existence in those days was almost fanatical. We knew the names of all the players with the senior clubs – clubs we had only heard of – and it was quite an event when on a Saturday evening the newspaper with the football results arrived.

Everyone gathered round to listen to them, and to talk about them, and when the 1905–06 rugby union All Blacks came over we followed their triumphant career with the fiercest interest. Everyone who knows anything about rugby football knows that their winning career was not checked until Wales beat them by a try scored by Teddy Morgan.

Now, Teddy Morgan's name became as well known in my district as that of any footballer, and we all used to talk about the wonderful type of football with which the All Blacks were revolutionising rugby. Their names stand as boldly in my memory as the names of men who have earned fame in the matches in which I have played.

Wallace, Hunter, Mynott, and Deans, who always said he scored a try in that historic match with Wales – when I was in New Zealand I was told that Deans' last words were "I scored that try" – were big men in that side, and so were Stead, Booth, and GW Smith, who afterwards played with Oldham, and who was an Olympic Hurdles Champion.

Then there were the big, strong fast forwards such as Gallaher, the captain, Glasgow, Cunningham, and two men who returned to England to play Northern Union football – Seeling and Johnstone.

All Blacks show possibilities.

Those 1905–06 All Blacks set a standard which showed the possibilities of the Rugby game, and, beyond all doubt, their influence counted for much, just as, a year or two later, Baskerville's Northern Union "All Blacks" came over to give new life to the Northern Union game.

In rugby football before the arrival of the 1904–05 All Blacks there had been two golden rules:
1. A man must never pass the ball in his own quarter.
2. The forwards must never let the ball come out anywhere near their own line – they must take it as far up the field as they could.

The rugby union All Blacks showed us that it was possible to score tries with combined movements from near their own line – they got tries the length of the field on that tour on which they scored 830 points to 39 and, what is more they showed that forwards used properly could be of the greatest assistance to the backs in passing.

They had forwards who could handle the ball and run with it like backs and they sounded the death knell of the heavy lumber-some forward who was only of use in struggling for possession of the ball.

All this was drummed into me as the tour of that successful team developed, and when the Welsh team which had such men as Winfield, Gwyn Nicholls, Teddy Morgan – quite a hero, Underbank way – W. Llewellyn, Owen, Pritchard and the others accounted for them, playing open football we began to realise in our little village that rugby football, in addition to taking a new lease on life, was to be faster and more attractive than ever it had been.

My first promotion

In 1905–06 I secured promotion from the Pump Hole Rangers to the Underbank side, chiefly because Underbank were a man short for their match with Milnsbridge. I turned out at centre threequarter and scored two tries, and the following week when Underbank had to meet Huddersfield "A", composed chiefly of men who had played in the first team and were professional players, I was chosen again.

I was weighing round about 10st, and I reckon I must have fancied my chance a bit. My father said I must not play, arguing that my bones were not set: but I did not say I would not play, and I slipped away quietly for the game.

Underbank gave Huddersfield 'A' a close game, and I, after scoring a try three parts the length of the field, returned home that evening expecting a bit of a "sousing" from father, but there was nothing said. He must have thought that, after all, I was big enough to look after myself, and when you come to think of it, you know, I suppose I have been fortunate in always being big enough for these tests.

Anyway, I played first class football for close upon 20 years and I never had a bone broken to know it. When I was near my end in the game, I found that two small bones in my right elbow had been chipped, but they never gave me any real trouble.

It was a curious thing, too, that I never played with my elder brother for Underbank. He had damaged an ankle before I got a place in the side, and by the time he was right to play again, I had moved on to Fartown. I saw the remainder of season 1905-6 through with Underbank and I remember that at the end of that season I had my first sight of a big game – the Northern Union Cup semi-final at Fartown, between Bradford and Batley when there were such men as Gomer Gunn, George Marsden, Jim Gath, Joe Oakland and Wattie Davies in action.

Two New Rules

In 1906–07 the rugby league game started with two new rules. The number of forwards was reduced from eight to six and it was ruled that the man knocking on the ball and playing it again should be allowed to carry on. We started in September, and then I never thought that at the age of 15 – my birthday anniversary had been celebrated the previous May – I should be playing senior football before the season was half-way through.

We went into the semi-final of the Halifax Charity Cup. First of all, we beat Raistrick and then we accounted for Birkhouse Rangers – I scored all the 10 points in the game – it was after the match at Moldgreen that I had the first intimation that there might be a chance for me in senior football.

The referee was the old Halifax and Yorkshire player, George Dickenson. He asked to be introduced to me, and when we had talked about the game for a bit, he wondered if I would like to play first-class football for Halifax.

I said I did not mind going anywhere for a game – in those days, young players were not tied to districts as they were in the Rugby

League until the other season – but nothing came of it. A long time afterwards, I heard that George had gone to the committee meeting at Thrum Hall on the Sunday morning and there he had told them about me. The Halifax people asked how old I was, and when he said 15, they decided I had better wait for a little while.

My football father

But on Monday there arrived at Underbank one of the most charming men I have known – the man who was to be my football father, Mr Joe Clifford, of Huddersfield, He asked me to sign for Huddersfield. I said I would not mind if he could make it right with father: but father said I ought to stay in junior football for a time, and that was all there was about it.

Mr Clifford would not take 'No' for an answer. He came to see us every night, and what is more, he saw both father and myself at work. In the end – on the following Friday night, as a matter of fact – his enthusiasm and persistence converted my father, who, when he came home from work said "Get yourself brightened up a bit: we are going down to your uncle's to see that chap from Huddersfield. He's been after me so much this week that I can't sleep and I can't work for him."

My uncle had the Druid's Hotel at Underbank, and there it was, after a bit of a talk, that Joe Clifford spread five golden sovereigns on the table, making them cover as much space as he could though he had no need to do that, for I thought it an enormous amount of money and there it was that I signed forms for Huddersfield.

2. First games at Fartown

When at my uncle's house in Underbank, Mr Joe Clifford, who right to his death a few years ago did so much work for the Huddersfield club – as much, I should imagine, as any other man – spread five golden sovereigns on the table, I said I would sign for Fartown on one condition – that I had a game with the first team straightaway.

I signed professional forms for Huddersfield on the night of Friday 2 November 1906, and I could not play for them on the Saturday because Underbank, my own team, had a cup tie with Slaithwaite Juniors. Underbank went down in that game, and the following Saturday, after a couple of trips to Fartown for training and practice, I played my first game with Huddersfield. Then, on 10 November 1906, I was $15^{1}/_{2}$.

The 'Claret and Gold' Jersey in those times was not the attractive affair it is now. The claret and gold bands were of even width and the jersey was made of a woollen material that made it uncomfortable.

A Hambrecht Memory

However, the match on 10 November 1906 was with Bramley at the Barley Mow. We won by 28 points to 11 and the referee was "Billy" McCutcheon, who had been asked by Mr Joe Clifford (I afterwards learned) to keep an eye on me. I could feel throughout the game that the referee was giving me every encouragement, and I learned when the game was finished that at half-time when Mr Clifford spoke to him about it, he said "The lad can look after himself".

That afternoon my opposite centre – I was in the Huddersfield middle along with Jim Davies – was a man who, while he was just past his prime, was still one of the strongest runners in the game – Hambrecht, whose weight was around 13 stones. My weight in those days had increased to close upon 11st, and in junior football it had, of course, been more than sufficient for me.

But the first time I went to tackle Hambrecht – I can feel the bump now when I think of it! If ever a youngster felt that he had been under a steam roller, I did. In junior football, if one looked hard enough at a man he would pass the ball. I tried the same trick with Hambrecht, and, when he made it clear that he was not going to be intimidated, I went on to tackle him, I am afraid, in a somewhat half-hearted sort of a way.

One knee hit me under the chin, the other whizzed past my face. I went down with a foot on my chest, and I realized at once that the making of a tackle in senior football was a vastly different thing from the making of a tackle in junior football.

Someone said "Get him sideways, don't face him." Whenever I had to tackle again that afternoon I dived at Hambrecht's ankles.

Jim Davies

That afternoon, as I have told you, my centre partner was Jim Davies, a man who, later on, was to have as much as anyone to do with the rise of Huddersfield. Jim, to put it perfectly plainly, was not at all pleased about having one so young in the middle with him, and it was not long before dear old Jim, who became one of my firmest friends, had something to say about football not being a game for babies. And there must, I imagine, have been just cause for this early comment.

I remember that in the opening minutes of the game I had to take a pass from Davies. Instead of the ball coming to me in a nice, gentle loop, as in junior football, it came like a shot from the mouth of a cannon. I had a good chance of scoring – I can see the opening now – but the ball crashed off my chest. It was not a good start.

Jagger, who afterwards went Bradford Northern, was the outside half, and I remember going to him just as a round-faced lad of 15 would go to a friendly looking player, and saying of Davies "isn't he a bad-tempered man." Jagger, who never failed to chaff me about this in later years, said "take no notice of him, get on with your laikin." And so I went on, managing in the second half to make a cut through which took me to near the posts for a try.

That was my first game. Afterwards I was never off the Huddersfield team sheet except for injury or illness. I never played with the second team either until, when right at the end of my career, I had a run with the second team in an effort to get myself fit to play with Huddersfield at Halifax in a charity cup competition.

On November 10, 1906, at Bramley, the Huddersfield team had Patchett at full-back, H. Moseley, who had returned to Huddersfield after Brighouse Rangers had disbanded, was on one wing, Davies and myself were in the centre, and Billy Kitchen was on the other wing. Jagger and a Welshman named Hopkins were the halves, and in the forwards there were such men as Wimpenny Brook, Ballinger, Langthorne, Ainley, Wilson and Arkle Hirst.

Bramley had Hogg at full-back, Whiteley and Hambrecht were their centres, Jones and Clarke, the halves, and in the strong pack you know, season after season. Bramley have managed to turn out a very useful sort of a pack, they had Binns, Neal, Clarke and Horn among the others.

First Fartown game

I was among those selected for the Halifax match the following Saturday; but, because it was a 'Derby' game, and because Halifax were then in their pomp, I did not play. I played against Leeds the Saturday afterwards. That was my first game at Fartown, and it was won by Leeds and I missed the following game with Keighley at Lawkholme.

That was the season in which Keighley got into the fourth position in the League, and with the side that was their best, until they got together the one they now have, they beat us by something like 27 points to 3. Then I went back into the side for the match with Hull Kingston Rovers at Fartown, scoring the two tries and the goal by which we won. From then onwards I had a regular place in the threequarter line.

One of the things that surprised me about that time was that I put on half a stone before the end of the season. The training at Fartown gave me strength and weight where I wanted it, around the hips and the thighs and before long I was turning the scale at somewhere near 12st. At all events, when I was 17 and I played in a Yorkshire trial match at Dewsbury, I weighed 12st, and I always said that my best playing weight was that I had when I went to Australia for the first time in 1914. Then I weighed 12 stones four pounds stripped.

But when I was 12 stones four pounds, I never looked to have anything like that weight, for I was tall and somewhat thin in the face; but I had the weight where I wanted it in the thighs round the hips, and I was strong in the chest. Do you know that I was so slim round the waist when I weighed 12 stones four pounds that Con. Burn, who came to Huddersfield from New Zealand, could, and frequently did span my waist with his two hands.

That body swerve

The body movement that was such an asset when I was running with the ball came from those sturdy hips and slim waist. I found I could sway this way and that way to baffle the men who sought to tackle me – the movement came automatically when there was danger near – and the more I think of it the more I am sure that the ability to make the body swerve came primarily from the slim waist.

I joined Huddersfield just about the time they began to look up after a lean spell. They had brought two or three men into the game from outside and the team was beginning to find steady feet. We went into the third round of the Northern Union Cup that season, and that was something Huddersfield had not done for a long, long time. In the third round we were beaten 17–9 at Fartown by Warrington, who went on to beat Oldham in the final at Wheaters' Field, Broughton, the first Northern Union Cup Final I saw.

In Northern Union football in those days there was far too much kicking. Clubs had not learned from the football played by Broughton Rangers' greatest team, nor had they taken to heart the lessons taught by the 1905 rugby union All Blacks. Now and then there would be passing in a straight forward sort of a way at Fartown but there was no manoeuvring to speak of and, generally it was kick, kick, kick, with plenty of following up and everybody relying on somebody making a mistake.

I used to think when I got home after the matches that there was an awful lot of energy wasted in Northern Union football. There were the forwards struggling as hard as they could for the ball, and as soon as they got it, the ball would be kicked down the field to the returned with interest by such full-backs as Gunn (Bradford) Metcalfe (Wakefield Trinity), Little (Halifax), and F. Young (Leeds). It all seemed very ridiculous.

The Fartown Revival

Then 1907-08 saw the real beginning of the Fartown revival, and that was, it is worth bearing in mind the season in which Baskerville's Northern Union 'All Blacks' came to England.

They were the phantom team – the team about which no one was sure and nothing was known until they actually arrived – and they had to learn the new game when they got here, much as the Frenchmen had to do last season.

However, to return to Fartown affairs we started our season with a match against Bradford, who have been compelled to leave Park Avenue and go the Athletic ground at Greenfield. Our only new man was a wing threequarter named Eddie Sykes, a local lad who had a reputation as a sprinter. Hopkins had not returned from Wales, and in his place at scrum-half we had Percy Holroyd.

We progressed a little in the first half of the season, but it was not until after Christmas that we began our decided advance. Then we were drawn against Broughton Rangers in the first round of the Cup. Before that Broughton game, we had to go down to Wales to play Merthyr and there we succeeded in persuading Jim Davies to return with us to Fartown. He took a position at off-half, we won at Halifax by 5–4. Jim scored a try and WD Llewellyn, who had been with Leeds, kicked a goal.

It was the first time Huddersfield had beaten Halifax for many a year and Jim's success in the off-half position led to him being kept in that berth. He stayed there in fact; until he joined the Army at the outbreak of war, and he was – I say this unhesitatingly – one of the best off-halves I ever saw. He set himself an enormously high standard, and he looked for everyone else setting themselves a high standard. I know, more than anyone else, of the part he played in the rise of Huddersfield.

At all events, between February 22 and the end of the season, Harry Wilson who was playing on the left wing, scored over 20 tries, and that simple fact, I say, tells of two things – the improvement of Fartown's football ideas and the ability of Harry Wilson, a winger of the Percy Eccles type, with a wonderful swerve. Unfortunately, he had an internal operation during the summer, and he was unable to reproduce that form.

In my next article I will tell of the lessons learned from the famous Broughton Rangers team and from Baskerville's pioneer team, and of the important part played by these lessons in our climb to fame.

Huddersfield 1907–08: Back: A. Bennett (trainer), W. Kitchin, W. Ainley, J. Barton, N. Micklethwaite, E. Balmforth, J. Cole, A. Swinden, H. Bennett (assistant trainer); front: P. Holroyd, E. Sykes, W. Patchett, J. Bartholomew, J. Jagger, H. Wagstaff. This team lost 17–11 to Hunslet at Fartown on 26 October 1907. (Courtesy Robert Gate)

Huddersfield RLFC 1908–09: Players: Back row: Binns, Ainley, Brook, Hirst, Charlesworth, Swinden; front: Davies, Jagger, Wagstaff, Kitchin, Holroyd, Bartholomew, Wrigley. (Courtesy Robert Gate)

3. Rise of Huddersfield – Wrigley, Gleeson and Co.

Points from this Article.

Possession is nine points of the law, especially in rugby league football ... When you have the ball, you ought to keep it: you cannot attack without it.

These are points made by Harold Wagstaff in the third instalment of the story of his football career. He started playing for Huddersfield when he was 15 years old. Two years later he played in his first county trial, and in that match at Crown Flatt he determined that he would not put his foot to the ball once he had got it in his hands. He went through the game without kicking the ball.

There was evidence of his faith in passing and running – evidence of the importance he attached to the lessons taught by Bakersville's 'All Blacks'. Remember that when he went with this firm resolution not to kick in this county trial he was 17 years old.

The more I think of it, the more I marvel at the way in which the greatest Huddersfield Northern Union team was built.

I have told how in the second half of season 1907–08 we were beaten by Broughton Rangers in the Northern Union Cup and how we went sailing through the remainder of that league season to gain, I believe, the fifth place in the league.

Our only defeat in that most successful league spell was sustained at Mount Pleasant, where Batley beat us by 13 points to 12, Wattie Davies landing a goal in the closing minutes of the match.

But to look fairly and squarely at the beginning of the rise of Huddersfield, one has I say, to go back to the beginning of 1907-08 to the second match of the tour made by Baskerville's Northern Union team. One has also to contemplate the way in which Broughton Rangers, then a little past their best, were playing football in those days. The work of both those sides had a marked influence on the type of football that was developed by the team in which I had the privilege to hold a place.

All the men in those teams understood to the full the advantage of possession. They knew that when they had the ball, they had a chance of doing something with it, and so, naturally enough they saw to it that they retained possession of that ball as long as they could. They were prepared to pass to their own men, but they were loath to kick because, to put it bluntly, they did not see the use of giving the ball to the other side.

This is a point I cannot emphasise too strongly in these days when there are greater opportunities than ever for passing and running in Rugby League football. There is the play the ball rule – but this is a matter with which I will deal later. All I need say at the moment is that Baskerville's team and Broughton Rangers taught me to the full the value of possession. They also taught me the importance of giving support to the man with the ball.

When they had it, they were prepared to go as far as they could go with it, but – and this is the vital point – they were always ready to part with it. Rather than go into a killing tackle with it, they would throw the ball wide – get rid of it anyhow – knowing, of course, that the odds were on one of their supporting colleagues getting his hands or his feet to it.

What's the use?

What, I ask, is the point of a forward or a back with the ball in his possession running smash into a tackle in the other side's half. He gets a bump and he deserves it, and, what is more, in taking the bump, he, holding on tight to the ball, gives the defence the opportunity of rallying.

It is far, far better for him to go into the tackle, and then let the ball go in the hope that his colleagues – and when a side is attacking, I say the odds always are on his colleagues – getting to the ball first. Anyway, the 'All Blacks' brought over by Baskerville knew to the full the advantage of such moves as these, and they brightened our games by introducing to it many attractive players and many attractive moves.

Forward and back alike, whenever they got the ball, they were prepared at any time to pass it to a man more favourably placed, and, forward and back alike, they were always sure of the right sort of support or backing up, whichever you like.

Many of them, it is true, were clever enough to know how to go into a tackle and leave themselves free to get rid of the ball as they liked, but even those who were not skilled enough for this move (which, I always think, distinguishes the able player from the ordinary one) were prepared as soon as they hit a tackle to let the ball go.

Basis of Fartown success

I must be forgiven for this lengthy digression, but the lesson had, I know, much to do with our success at Fartown; and, what is more, the lesson is one which might be studied by many men who are playing in first-class rugby football in these times.

The second half of season 1907–08 had rescued hope of a successful future at Fartown, and, as the Huddersfield Committee was in a progressive frame of mind, there was encouragement for the men who carried the colours of the Claret and Gold.

Edgar Wrigley, one of the 'stars' brought over by Baskerville, was signed on by the Huddersfield club, and he was there very early on in season 1908–09 to take his place in the back division. Wrigley stayed at Fartown until Tommy Gleeson took his place, and he had much to do with the placing of Huddersfield on the Northern Union map. He was one of the many members of Baskerville's team who came back to England to carry on the grand work started by their team. Indeed, two men, GW Smith, who is now the trainer of the Oldham rugby league team, and Lance Todd, who is the secretary-manager of the Salford club, remained in England all the time, and I believe I am right in saying that they have never been to New Zealand since they left it with that so-called phantom team.

Lance Todd played at five-eight in Baskerville's side, and I, for one, shall never forget the tries he scored when the tour team beat us at Fartown. But before we go any further into this matter let us think for a second or two of the men supplied to Northern Union football by that team. Turtill, the full-back, and Kelly, the scrum-half, went to St Helens, Rowe, the threequarter, went to Leeds, Lavery went to Leeds and then to Leigh, Wrigley, Con Burn and Trevarthan went to Huddersfield, Todd went to Wigan and G.W. Smith went to Oldham.

There are the names of nine men whose football was to make a lasting impression with the clubs with whom they played, because they believed all the time in giving the ball plenty of light and air, because they believed in passing and manoeuvring and because they believed in keeping the ball among their own men once thy had secured possession of it.

In short, they knew the value of team work. They knew that team work could do everything; that brilliant individualism counted for little.

Hull KR the exception

You know when I look back through the years that I have been connected with the game, I can only think of one team that achieved any amount of consistent success with ideas contrary to those laid down above. The Hull Kingston Rovers team which in the early years after the war kept taking this trophy and that trophy and going through to this final and that final had none of these ideas; but it had a team spirit based on different principles.

That Hull Kingston side had behind it the gloriously sound full-back play of Osborne, it had a resolute strong fairly fast and accurate handling threequarter line, and it had a pack of forwards who knew how to support in their daring and dashing following-up the kicking of such men as Osborne and Cook. There was team work of a different kind, but mighty effective team work all the same. What is more that Hull Kingston back division in which there were such men as Harris, Austin, Cook and the others could open and pass with the best in a straight-forward fashion.

Wrigley's first game

Anyway, to get back to the very important arrival of Edgar Wrigley at Fartown. He got there in September, 1908, and he played his first game for Huddersfield on Honley Feast Saturday, turning out against the Hornets at Rochdale. He was fly-half that day, Billy Kitchin and I were the centres, Percy Holroyd the scrum-half, and Eddie Sykes and Harry Wilson were the wings.

Now in those days, Honley Feast was the big holiday in Huddersfield. The mills would close down on Friday night until Wednesday morning – we had no August holidays in Huddersfield in those times – and so, of course, we always had a full holiday programme at Fartown.

On the Monday, we played Swinton, Edgar Wrigley taking the left wing berth, and on the Tuesday, we played Wigan at Fartown, Edgar Wrigley taking the centre berth in partnership with me. It was the first time for many years that Huddersfield and Wigan had met in league football, and the fixture had only come about because we had finished in the fifth position the previous season. We lost by 10 points to 3 after a grand game; but we played our part in the game, and that was all we hoped to do against a Wigan back division in which there were such men as Sharrock, the full-back, Miller and Leytham, the wings, Todd and Jenkins, the centres, and Johnny Thomas and Gleave, the halves.

We were improving.

We beat Trinity at Wakefield in the first round of the Yorkshire Cup – Trinity had backs of the calibre of Metcalfe, Simpson, Lynch, McPhail, Bennett, Kershaw, and Newbould, with Crossland and company in the forwards – and then we were beaten at home by Batley. But still we did not care about the defeat because we felt all the time that we were on the right track with our football and that we had only to persevere at the open and quick backing-up game to succeed.

My first county trial

That season, when I was 17 years old, I had my first trial for Yorkshire, and I have a story to tell about the Probables and Possibles game at

Dewsbury which will tell more than anything else can of the deep impression made upon me by the Northern Union 'All Blacks'.

I had so much confidence in the style of football that I thought the best and most profitable, that I determined on my way to that match not to kick the ball once. And not once in that game did I put my foot to the ball after handling it.

Maybe, of course, I kicked the ball in a dribble, but once the ball touched my hands, I kept it there until I passed it. I always attribute my success in my first trial for Yorkshire to that resolution not to kick. Why should a threequarter back, who is there for attack, kick the ball? His job is to run with it, and, in running, make play for colleagues who also are prepared to run and handle. They say that possession is nine points of the law. It ought to be all that, and a little more in rugby league football.

A ball kicked to the opposition is a ball wasted

Next week I will tell of the arrival at Fartown of Rosenfeld, Clark, Major Holland, and a few others, of the completion of the side that broke Wigan's scoring record of over 700 points in a season, and of a disastrous season for me.

A Letter from Wales

Barry Dock, Glamorgan,
Dear Harold, – you will certainly be surprised to hear from me, but when I opened the Sports Post *the other Saturday, I get it sent to me in Wales, and have done ever since my playing days ended – I saw the start of the story of your football career. It brought back happy memories, and I know that it will bring back happy memories of pleasant days to many other old players.*
I look forward to the remainder of your reminiscences, and I may say that many of my friends down here are looking forward just as keenly. When I showed them the first of your stories they were vastly interested, for, though they had never seen you play, they know all about you. They are always interested when I tell them about those happy football days in the North before the war.
Yours faithfully
FRANK YOUNG (Leeds)

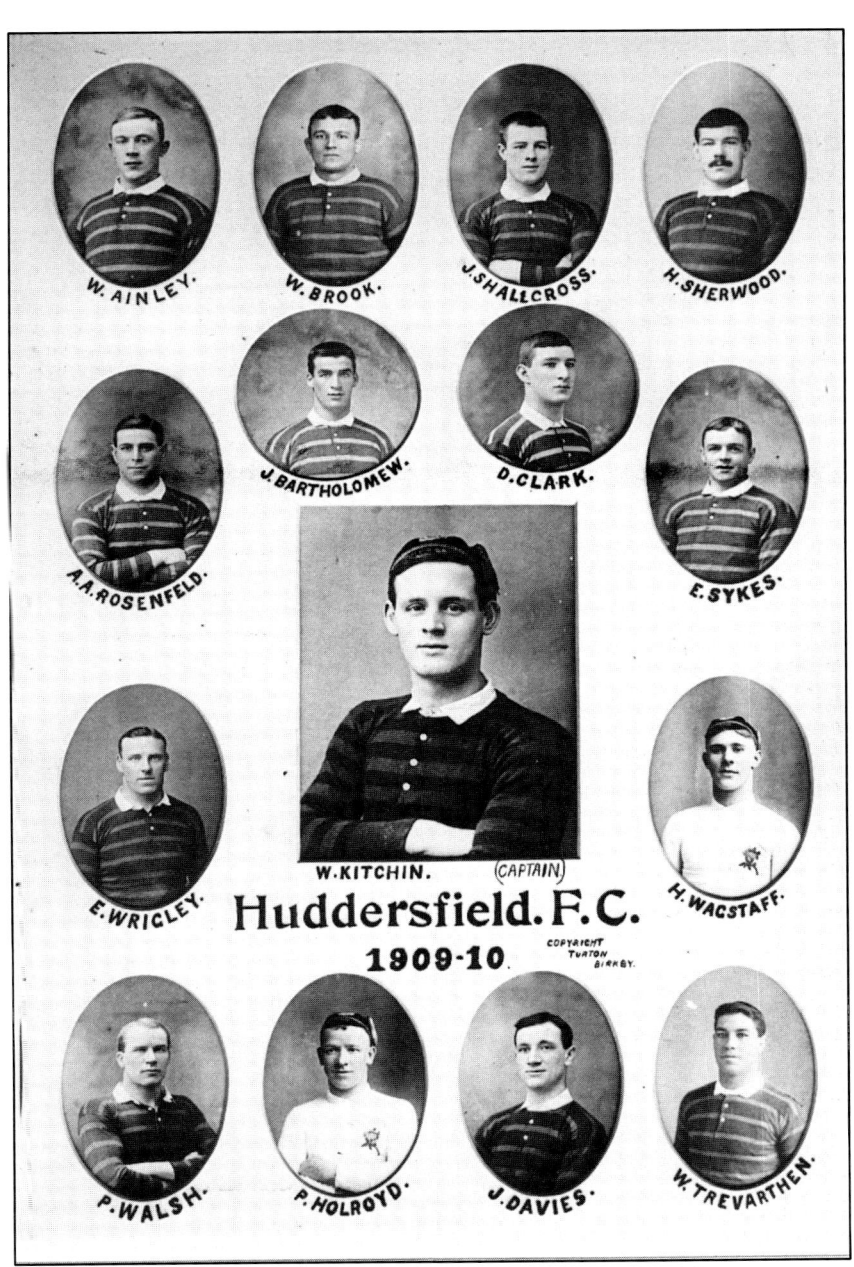

Huddersfield RLFC 1909-10 (Courtesy Robert Gate)

4. Huddersfield build up a great side

It was in season 1908–09 that I played in my first county trial, and in that season, I played in my first county and international matches. At Fartown, Yorkshire met and beat a Cumberland side which had fine footballers of the type of James Lomas, W Eagers and Joe Ferguson in its ranks; but the Lancashire side, a great one, beat us on one of the Manchester grounds.

In those days, a man could play for the county in which his club was situated, no matter what his birth qualification, and so it came about that in the Lancashire team that day there were many brilliant outsiders. Their back division, which will give you an idea of the worth of the combination, had Gifford at full back, Leytham, Jenkins, Todd and GW Smith in the threequarter line, and Jolley, of Runcorn, was one of the half-backs.

In their forwards were such hefty stalwarts as Ramsdale, Shugars and Bert Avery – men who were to have a big hand in the success of the first England NU team to Australia in 1910 – and their forwards, as well as their backs, taught us quite a lot that afternoon. But I only had an eye for the work of the backs for the beautifully straight running of the Lancashire centres and the way in which they went straight through to the full-back before throwing out the ball to their fast wing-men.

An important match in my football education was that Roses battle. The brilliant Lancashire football made an impression on me, and so did the lunch and dinner functions before and after the match. Everyone sat down friendly and happy, everyone carried the badge of his county – the Yorkshiremen had white roses, and the Lancastrians had red roses – and I know that I left Manchester that evening a very happy youngster of 17, and that despite the fact that we had been beaten.

Appeal of county matches

I had seen another side of the Northern Union game, and I was very pleased with it. Always, after that, County football made a great appeal to me. It did not matter that the pay for a county match was much less than club pay – I would willingly have played without pay: the honour was enough for me. The football was of the very best in those days, too, when county caps were regarded as something that really did count.

There was the first Australian NU team in England that season, a side which provided many fine players for the Northern Union clubs, and a side with a grand idea of the game, and that though their playing record was not at all a successful one. Rosenfeld one of the finest wing men I have seen, was a member of that team, and so were Sid Deane, Dan Frawley, Devereux, Courtney and Craig.

Many of them returned to play with success in England, and so spread their style of football. More and more, as I go back through memories, do I realise the importance of the part played by Australians and New Zealanders in the development of the game over here.

My first game for England was against the Australians on 1 January 1909, and that match like my first for the county, was played at Fartown. Dally Messenger was unable to play for the Australians that day, when their full-back was Bolewski, the threequarters, Frawley, Deane, Devereux and Heidke; their halves Conlon and Halloway and their forwards O'Malley, Abercrombie, Burdon, Pearce, Courtney and Walsh.

We had Gilford of Barrow, at full-back, Tyson and Batten on the wings; Lomas was in the centre with me; Newbould and Holroyd were our halves and in our forwards were Jukes, Higson, Smith, Longworth Mann, and Robinson.

Two caps at age of 17

With a county cap and an international cap at the age of 17, I reckoned that things were going nicely for me, and, best of all, I was learning from all the men with whom I played, Jimmy Lomas taught me quite a lot in that international with the Australians.

The season did not end as well as we had hoped it would at Fartown – injuries and the like retarded our development – and we had to be content with the seventh or eighth position in the league and the glory of the game we played with Wigan at Fartown in the third round of the Rugby League Cup.

They talk about that struggle in Huddersfield and Wigan to this day. The crowd was a record for Fartown at the time, and the match was a glorious affair, with fast and clever attacking, and, in the end, a draw of 10–10. Lance Todd was the hero. His defence in the second half when we were all out was brilliant. I can see him now cutting across to first one wing and then the other to hold our fast men. Our interest in the Cup closed in the replay at Central Park.

However, before the end of that season, we knew that Albert Rosenfeld, who while wearing the colours of the Claret and Gold was to create a try-scoring record that still stands – a record that will take a lot of beating – had been added to the Fartown strength. In addition, there were such men as Elijah Watts from Leeds, and Sherwood, from Hull Kingston Rovers, to give extra power to the Fartown pack.

Since the first Sherwood joined Huddersfield from Craven Street, there always has been a Sherwood on the club's register.

Douglas Clark made himself known to Fartown folk before the end of the season, too. A match was played at Fartown with a side of Cumberland Colts, and out of that Colts XIII Clark who then was close upon 18 – his birthday anniversary comes 17 days before mine – was picked. I believe that Douglas, who in those days weighed roundabout 13 stones, actually signed forms for Huddersfield on the day that Wakefield Trinity beat Hull in the Cup Final at Headingley.

A 'graze' at Bramley

Anyway, he was there with all the others at the start of 1909–10, a season of which we at Fartown had the highest hopes. I little knew what was in store for me when we took the field at Bramley in the opening match. We won fairly comfortably, and at the time I thought little about the damaged knee I sustained when I dived in a futile effort to prevent May, the fast Bramley scrum-half, from scoring a try.

I got him all right; but he was a strong runner, and he went over the line dragging me behind him. His path took him over a bare patch – they played cricket at the Barley Mow in the summer in those times and the bare patch had been caused by the batsmen's feet – and there I grazed my knee.

I thought nothing to it at the time, played in the two following games, with Broughton Rangers whom we beat by 30 points and Leeds, over whom at Headingley we gained a dramatic victory with Wrigley kicking a wonderful goal from halfway in the closing minutes.

And then came the blow. I was down at Fartown for training when they discovered I had a temperature of 104. I was rushed home, doctors and specialists were called in, it was touch and go whether I lived, and finally, I was taken to a private ward in Leeds Infirmary, where Lord Moynihan, then Mr Berkeley Moynihan, administered the treatment that, against odds, saved my life.

While I was in the Infirmary a keen follower of the Hunslet club, who was attending that ward as an out-patient, asked permission to pop in my little room and have a talk with me. He talked about football at first, and that was all right. But then he began to tell me about the number of men who had died in my bed when he was an in-patient in the big ward. I managed to get rid of him, and I saw to it through the sister that the enthusiastic Hunslet follower never visited me in that room again.

A bad season for me

As promised, I was moved to the big ward for company, and then another blow fell. On the day I had the first real meal I had had for weeks – the chicken was champion! – my temperature shot up to 104 again. That night I slept in the Seacroft Isolation Hospital, a victim of diphtheria. So, you will see that I know very little about the football at Huddersfield in the first half of season 1909–10.

Rosenfeld took my place in the centre – then the three-quarters were Sykes, Wrigley, Rosenfeld and Kitchin – and that team went in triumph to the Yorkshire Cup Final in which Batley were beaten. So, it happened that I was out of the team which won the first Cup in my time at Fartown. Injury and ill-luck, however, dogged that side. Wrigley had to undergo an operation for appendicitis, and there was more disarrangement of the threequarter line. Tommy Grey was secured from Halifax to play at half-back.

The Rugby League Cup competition opened; we beat Oldham by 2–0. I watched that game from the stand and then we were drawn at home with Ebbw Vale. It was thought to be a good thing for Huddersfield, but Ebbw Vale were the masters and the deserving winners 8–0, and there was little left for us in that season. That Ebbw Vale defeat is reckoned the biggest shock ever sustained by Huddersfield in Cup football, and they still talk about it in the town.

I still hoped to get a place in the first team for Australia and I started training a little too soon. A knock reminded me that I had been fortunate indeed to escape from the threat of blood-poisoning, and I had to take things very easily until the start of 1910–11.

Bartholomew and Davies went from Huddersfield on that 1910 Australian tour, and with their return, and with side which was equipped as no previous Huddersfield side had been equipped, we prepared in the belief that we were in for our best season ever.

Hope deferred

John Willie Higson, Fred Longstaff, Trevarthan, Paddy Walsh, Con Burn, Sherwood, Clark, Swinden and all the forwards were there, including the great Ben Gronow. Stanley Moorhouse was ready for the threequarter line for which there were Rosenfeld, Kitchin, Todd, Wrigley and myself. At half-back, we had Jim Davies and Tommy Grey and Major Holland was ready for a chance at full-back.

Beyond going to the final of the Yorkshire Cup – Wakefield beat us at Headingley – we did little in the first half of the season. Indeed, when the mid-season balance was taken, we found that we had lost 14 of 21 games in which we had played. The hopes of the back combination had not been realised. I was still feeling the effects of the previous season's illness. Wrigley had not got over his appendix operation, others were troubled with their injuries, and the returned tourists had not settled, as is so frequently the case when a man starts playing what is his third season in a row.

The team could not find its feet, and that was all there was about it. This, however, was not satisfactory to the Fartown executive, and there came a time when they called all the players to a meeting at Fartown. Then they said plainly that the time had come for a change and that they intended having it, "choose how."

The turning point

They gave us to understand definitely that in the following Saturday's match with Bramley – have you noticed how Bramley keep popping up at important points in this story? – we would be judged on form and not on reputation and that if form did not fit with reputation many men would find themselves in the second team.

The result was that 30 points were scored against Bramley, and that started a run of League success that went through the remainder of the season. The only match we lost was that with Wigan in the Cup – it was another grand game – and, through this league rally, we climbed well into the top half of the table, breaking Wigan's League scoring record by making over 800 points, of which two thirds were made after the Bramley match.

The framework of our best team was almost complete. The skill was there, the ideas were there and the men capable of developing to the full those ideas were there also.

5. "Scientific Obstruction" was born at Bramley

In season 1911–12 Mr Charles Ford, the manager of the Australian team which toured England that season, described Huddersfield as the finest club side in the world.

He paid this tribute to us at the dinner which followed the Huddersfield – Australia match at Fartown, a match we won by 21 points to 7. That afternoon, during which we scored five tries against what I consider to be the soundest Australian team sent to this country, we gave what many Huddersfield people regard as the best exhibition ever given by a side wearing the colours of the 'Claret and Gold'.

The Australians were a grand lot, too, and the game, as I remember it, was one of this finest, if not actually the best, in which I took part. Forwards handled and ran like backs – it was rugby league football at its best.

Huddersfield RLFC 1912–13: Winners of the Northern Rugby League, the Challenge Cup and the Yorkshire League. Back: T. Gleeson, T. Grey, J. Rogers, A. Bennett (trainer), J. Davies, M. Holland; middle: A.A. Rosenfeld, E. Wrigley, H. Wagstaff (captain), S. Moorhouse, G. Todd, W.F. Kitchin; front: D. Clark, J.W. Higson, F. Longstaff, A. Lee, B. Gronow, J. Chilcott, A. Swinden. (Both pictures courtesy Robert Gate)

Huddersfield RLFC 1912–13: Winners of the Northern Rugby League, the Challenge Cup and the Yorkshire League. Back: T.H. Grey, M. Sutcliffe (Committee), Joe Clifford (chairman); standing: A. Bennett (trainer), A. Lee, John Clifford (vice-president), D. Clark, A. Swinden, E. Wrigley, F. Longstaff, J.W. Higson, J. Chilcott, B. Gronow, H. Bennett (assistant trainer); sitting: M. Holland, J. Davies, H. Wagstaff (captain), T. Gleeson, G. Todd, S. Moorhouse; front: A.A. Rosenfeld, J. Rogers. The trophies are the Northern Rugby League Championship trophy, Challenge Cup and Yorkshire League trophy.

That was my first season as captain of Huddersfield, though in the last three matches of 1910–11, I had, when Percy Holroyd was hurt, taken over the captaincy. That season, too, I played for the first time on a winning Huddersfield side in a cup final. We beat Hull KR in the final for the Yorkshire Cup at Wakefield on the Saturday before the historic game with the Australians at Fartown. Now I have two memories of that game with the Australians. The first has to do with the third of our tries, scored just after half-time, and the second concerns the tackling in which Bert Gilbert and I were concerned.

A great try

We will look at the try first of all. Tommy Grey got the ball from the scrummage at our 25 and went to the blind side as though he intended to make play for Stanley Moorhouse. He 'dummied' and doubled in to pass inside to Douglas Clark, who had left the pack to go with him. Clark passed to Davies, who had come up on the other side of the scrummage and Jim let me have the ball.

I sent it on to Wrigley and so it reached Rosenfeld, who shot down the touch-line. But Rosenfeld was covered by the magnificent Australian defence – that despite the fact that our passing had been quick and progressive – and he returned the ball to Wrigley, who in due course, let me have it again.

I found Jim Davies in support and gave him the ball, and he turned to find three forwards ready to carry on. So, the ball passed through the hands of the forwards to Moorhouse who shot over for the score at the corner.

Three of us had the ball twice in that movement in which 12 passes were made. If my memory is right, only Bartholomew, the full-back and two of the forwards did not have a hand in that passing.

Tackling!

I played opposite to Bert Gilbert that afternoon. I had many tussles with him in Australia and in English football, when he threw in his lot with Hull; but none of them compared with the deadly keenness of our duel that afternoon.

Gilbert, I always thought, was the hardest running Australian centre the game has known. There we were, two fit and strong young men, each as determined as could be, to meet the other fair and square in this battle. He tackled me and I tackled him. We went into it with all the power and speed we had at our command because each of us knew that the tackle had to be made full on, and without a fraction of a second's delay.

At the end of that game my ears were puffed up like a boxer's, and the top of the left one was torn –you can see the mark now. It was all as fair as could be – just honest-to-goodness tackling.

In those days I weighed 12 stones, 4 pounds, and Gilbert would weigh something like 12 stones 10 pounds. I can still feel the shock of those tremendous tackles when I think about them.

I played in test football for the first time that season – I was in the side that played the Australians at Newcastle and in the side that played Australians at Edinburgh – but there will be opportunity to tell of my test matches experiences later. In the meantime, there is the continued rise of Huddersfield to think of.

We lost no more than five matches that season, but we had one terrible blow, for, when we felt certain that we would take the four cups, we lost to Oldham in the third round of the Cup. For that match, in which we were beaten 2–0, thousands walked from Huddersfield over the top to Watersheddings. There was a coal strike at the time, and all manner of vehicles were brought into use to get the followers of the Fartown club to Oldham.

A blow at Oldham

They had a fine side at Oldham then, and, with their big men, they always were dangerous opponents for us. Anlezark, Jimmy Lomas, Alf Wood, the full-back, Avery, Ferguson, Smith and Longworth were among their top notchers. Things got a bit warm and 'Bob' Robinson, the referee, issued a warning at one point that the next time anything happened someone would go off.

Longstaff suffered; but, though we were a man short, we did most of the attacking against a glorious defence. We had one great chance, but Tommy Grey tried to drop a goal when he might have gone through for a try, and that was the end of it.

In that game, for the only time in my long career, I felt that someone really had tried to hurt me. I was going with the ball and just preparing to make a body swerve to beat one man when another stepped in from nowhere at all to take my legs. He lifted me in the tackle and another defender came along to get hold of my head.

In that position, when I was suspended between two tacklers, a third man – I never saw him, so I have never been able to name him – came along to inflict an injury which caused me to yell with pain. Anyway, we lost the match 2–0 and with it went our 'Four Cups' ideas.

The Yorkshire League was a walk-over and in the final for the League Championship we played Wigan at Halifax. Wrigley, troubled again with his stomach, was an absentee, and I had Kitchin in the centre with me.

Rattling knees

I had been in bed all the week with my first dose of influenza. I did not get out of bed until the Friday afternoon, and I was as weak as a kitten. When I travelled with the team from Huddersfield to Halifax, I had no more idea than the man in the moon of taking part in the game.

We got to Thrum Hall about threequarters of an hour before the kick-off, and Bennett, the trainer, asked me to have a run to see what I felt like. I went out on the Halifax cricket ground, very doubtful about it all, made the run requested by Bennett, and then heard Bennett say that I'd do.

So, I turned out, and for the first quarter of an hour, it felt as though my legs were not attached to me. When I stood to take a ball, I could feel my knees rattling together and, frankly, I knew very little about the first half of the game – very little except that Charlie Seeling, Wigan's loose forward, was giving a wonderful exhibition of tackling, most of which seemed to be directed against me.

Those who remember Charlie Seeling will remember that marvellous diving tackle he had. Now I firmly believe that Seeling's tackling knocked life into me. The second half was a grand battle, victory was ours, but after a bit of dinner at the George, I was glad to get home again and crawl into bed.

That season of 1911–12, in which we won the Yorkshire Cup, the Yorkshire League, and, for the first time, the Northern Rugby League Championship, was the season in which we developed the move which created so much controversy. Others described it as scientific obstruction; we at Fartown preferred to talk of it as the standing pass.

It was just before the Australian match to which I have referred in the article that we thought about and perfected the standing pass movement. The idea came as the result of a pure accident, arising out of an extraordinary set of circumstances in a match with Bramley – Bramley again!

Birth of an idea

We were playing the 'Villagers' in one of the rounds of the Yorkshire Cup, when Jim Davies and I worked by accident the first standing pass. The ball was light, there was gusty and troublesome wind, the ground was dry, and most important of all, Bramley had a forward named McManus who, given a certain amount of liberty by the referee, was a positive nuisance to Tommy Grey, our scrum-half.

Tommy that afternoon had had his fingers rapped three or four times by McManus, who was winging from the pack ever so quickly and, what with this and the wind and the light ball, which bobbed about on the ground in a most disconcerting fashion, he could not give Jim Davies the customary accurate passes.

Jim began to talk in his fiery Welsh fashion about the quality of the service he was getting, and, after one or two passes had shot along the ground in front of Jim, who always stood fairly deep, I began to step in ready to take them. Once or twice I got the ball and tried to go through with it, only to be held by the keen Bramley tackling.

Then, towards the end of the first half, a shocking sort of pass came out, bouncing on the ground a long way in front of Jim, I was half prepared for something like that happening, and I went in to get the ball before the Bramley backs swooped on it.

Then I found that Jim had taken up a position on the outside. "I'm here," he shouted, and I simply turned round to pass the ball to him. Straightway he had half of the field to work in. With Kitchin he went up to the full-back, slipped a dummy as well as he could slip one, and walked over under the posts.

Development

On the way back from the try Jim said he thought there was something in the move, and we decided to wait for an opportunity to work it again. We tried it a time or two in the match, decided that in view of its success, there was reason for the practice and development of it, and so the standing pass was born.

I should say that the majority of the tries we scored that season came from that move, the first glimmering of which arose out of those unusual circumstances in the Bramley match. They called it scientific obstruction. We called it scientific attack.

All that happened was that there was a quick changing of position between Davies and myself, the perfect timing of a pass, and there, at once a couple of defenders were cut out and an extra attacker sent away with the ball.

There was no obstruction. What could I do when I had passed the ball? I could not rise into the air; I could not sink through the ground. I had a vital part in the movement, so how could I be guilty of obstruction? If there was any obstruction it was committed on me, for, invariably, I after passing the ball was cut out of taking any further part in the movement.

Four yards straight

As we developed the move, we restricted its use so that we only called upon it now and then when I (the left centre) was first centre to Davies.

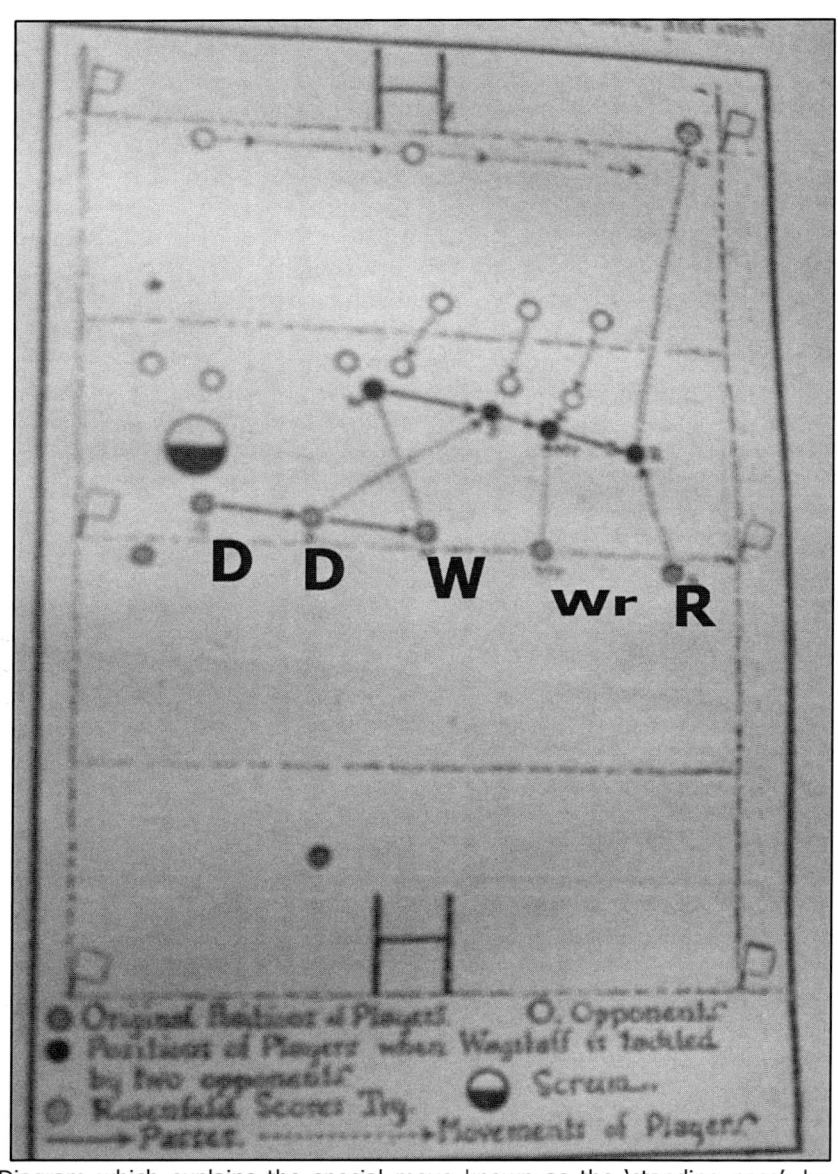

Diagram which explains the special move known as the 'standing pass', by means of which Wagstaff and the Huddersfield halves and threequarters non-plussed and held opposing teams some yards back, and which is occasionally practised even now [1921]. It aroused considerable controversy at the time of its inception. In this diagram, G stands for Grey, scrum-half, D for Davies, stand-off, W for Wagstaff, Wr for Wrigley, and R for Rosenfeld, right winger. (Diagram and caption from *All Sports Illustrated Weekly*)

Then the ball would flash out from Grey to Davies, and, without delay, Jim would let me have it. Ready for the ball I would be on the move nicely when Jim hit me with one of his perfect passes, and I would go dead straight for four yards or so – until I was opposite the scrummage which by then would not have broken up.

Then, according to the way in which I weighed up the situation, I would either turn round and pass to Jim, who would be on the outside of me and moving at top speed, or else I would, while standing and facing the opposition, pop the ball over my shoulder into Jim's hands.

If I saw that the centre opposite me was coming for me, I turned round and sought to meet the shock of his tackle with my right hip. If I saw that the tackle was coming from my other flank I would face it, seek to meet the tackle with the hip, and slip the ball over my shoulder to Davies.

A successful move for the side – of that there was no doubt – but it cost me a great deal of pain. I have come out of matches with my hips so sore that I could not put my hands on them, with hips so sore that the weight of my clothes seemed to hurt and sleep that night was almost an impossibility.

The secret of the success of the move is to be found in the straight dash of four yards or so that I made with the ball; but this is a matter I will discuss next week, when I will tell of the efforts that were made to check it, of the only man who did put a stop to it, and of the only men I have seen duplicate the move with success.

6. Finest team that ever played at Fartown

I have told of the development of the standing pass move which earned so many tries for us and which aroused, so much controversy among those who were pleased to term it 'scientific obstruction'.

I have tried to stress the vital importance of the straight run of four yards or so made by the centre on receiving the ball from the stand-off half. Without that dash of four yards straight and true into the heart of the opposition defence, the move cannot be made to pay.

You remember how we worked it in the brightest days of the 'Claret and Gold'. Tommy Grey slung out the ball as fast as he could to Jim Davies, standing, as he always did, fairly deep. Jim Davies shot the ball to me, and, by that time, of course, I was on the move. I went as hard as I could for those four yards or so, and then, when I had pulled in the defenders, I would turn round, face Davies crossing behind the position I had taken up and give the ball to him.

The quickness with which it was executed generally left Davies, Wrigley and Rosenfeld with any amount of room in which to work, and, more than that it usually cut out the fast winging forwards of the opposition, for they were on the other side of the little crowd of which I was the centre – I more often than not was on the ground with two or three men on top of me.

Four yards and a bump

In going that straight four yards – I aimed in that dash to get level with the scrummage before I turned round to pass to Davies – I made the ground and opened the way for the right wing to profit by Davies's link with me.

And I tell all this in the hope that clubs will be tempted to try and make use of the move which produced so many tries for Huddersfield.

The need is for a scrum half able to find with complete accuracy his off-half, for that off-half to be ready to send the ball on to the first centre, and for the first centre to be strong enough and prepared to go that important distance forward and take, when he gets there, the buffeting that is surely there for him.

Sometimes we see the standing pass tried in these days, but it is worked with the man who turns round never leaving the position at which he received the pass – the vital bit of ground has not seen gained. The result is that the first man has to run tremendously hard to get the ball from the player who delivers the standing pass and he runs to no profit at all. The covering defence moves with him and, more often than not, his side unless they have an enormous speed advantage, lose ground.

Only once since we finished have I seen the move exploited as we used to exploit it, and that was in a match between Warrington and Halifax at Thrum Hall. Flynn, the Warrington off-half, linked with 'Billy' Dingsdale, after Dingsdale had taken the ball from Flynn and gone straightforward. As soon as Dingsdale turned to make the pass, I shouted with joy that it was a try – there was nothing, save deplorable passing that could have stopped the score.

Only one man stopped us

At the time we employed the move, there was only one man who put a check on it. Billy Batten when he was in the middle for Hull, saw the way to do the trick I'm not going to reveal Batten's tactics. They were fair, and they were effective but I think it better simply to tell of the move and the way in which it was worked in the hope that some of our clubs will make an effort to use it.

It is difficult enough to play constructive football as it is, without adding to the difficulties by telling of the moves which work the other way. Hull Kingston Rovers made a big effort to put a stop to it in one match in which we scored something like 30 points. They set a couple of men to care for Davies alone, and they succeeded in worrying Jim quite a lot, but in caring for Jim they unwittingly opened another avenue. For instance, there came a time in that game when I went straight forward in my short dash and turned round in readiness to pass to Davies only to find that Jim was not there.

He had taken his watch-dogs with him, and he shouted "Turn round again Harold and score". I followed his advice, turned around again, and found that the way to the line was as clear as could be. Indeed, running backwards I could have scored that try.

But Billy Batten, who was a great footballer, approached the situation from another angle, and he really did strangle that move. I don't think I knew a man who was a harder tackler than Billy. When he set himself for the job, he went into it with every ounce he had got. He just put all his weight and power in the tackle, and when he got you – well you felt as though a cyclone had hit you.

The 'Pass Word'

We worked the standing pass very successfully in one match at Wigan, scoring in the end something like 23–3. Wigan, keen as mustard to put a stop to us, got the first try, and they held us so well that it was not until we had been playing about a quarter of an hour that an opportunity came for the unfolding of the move.

Then Jim Davies said, as he always did before we tried it, "How do you feel?" I said "Right," and prepared for it. As I got moving with the ball, Bert Jenkins from one side, and Johnny Thomas, from the other side, came into me with a smash; but just as I began to go in the tackle, I got the ball away to Jim. There I was underneath Jenkins and Thomas. Johnny, who stammered a little when he was excited, cried "Now then get up and play that ... ball".

I replied, pointing down the field, "Look". And there was Jim Davies, who had given one dummy, just passing to Rosenfeld, to send the winger sailing round the full-back. Johnny Thomas's comments can be passed over.

There was another instance in that match of the excellent standard of our passing in those days. Moorhouse got moving on the wing, and the wingman and Sharrock, the full-back, set themselves out for a killing tackle. They timed their tackle, as they reckoned, to perfection, and Stanley went into the straw with them. But when they sorted themselves out, they discovered to their sorrow, that Moorhouse, as he was going into touch, had slipped the ball back inside to me. All there was left for me to do was to run to the line and touch down.

Some of Wagstaff's Huddersfield team-mates

Top: Douglas Clark
Middle: Ben Gronow
Bottom: Stanley Moorhouse
(All courtesy Robert Gate)

Top: Johnny Rogers
Middle: Albert Rosenfeld
Bottom: Gwyn Thomas
(All courtesy Robert Gate)

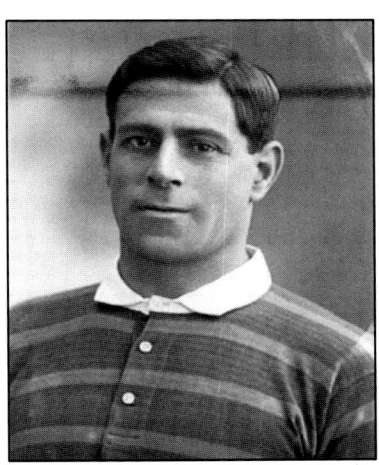

The success of the standing pass move was, of course one reason why so many of our tries were scored on the right wing. As I have told we only worked it when I, the left centre, was first centre to Jim Davies, the off half.

But we had many moves in those happy days – we were always trying to do some manoeuvring always seeking something out of the ordinary. And I can tell you that no one was more disappointed than Huddersfield when we won through the mistakes of the other people.

Finely balanced side

Our side was beautifully balanced, and beautifully built too – don't forget that. We had weight as well as speed all the way round. As a matter of fact, I believe that only Major Holland and Sherwood of that side failed to get international honours, and the point to remember is that most of our men earned their international honours while they were with the club.

Major Holland was a grand full-back for us. He could catch and he could kick, and, what is more, he could run into attack better than many were prepared to give him credit for being able to do. Then one the wings, we had Rosenfeld and Stanley Moorhouse, with Kitchen fit and able to take either position, or to go in the centre if there was needed. Now Moorhouse and Rosenfeld each weighed about 12 stones. Rosenfeld was a half second man on the track, and when in football gear, Moorhouse who, because he had to wear raised insteps in his football boots, could never train in pumps, was almost as fast.

Wrigley weighed 13½ stones and was about as fast as I was, and I in those days weighed 12 stones four pounds. I never did anything better than 11½ seconds, and there were forwards in the side who were faster than me. Jim Davies, who weighed 11 stones, and who was wiry and tough, was much the same speed Wrigley and myself, and Tommy Grey, whose football weight was 10 stones – if he fell, say to 9 stones 12 pounds he would say he owed the scales a couple of pounds – was, I should say, the slowest man in the side.

Tommy Grey's skill

But Tommy Grey was a lovely scrummage half back. I never saw a man more skilled then he in the art of passing a ball. He could start as though he intended passing it this way, and then, all in the same beautiful sweep he would bring his arms back and throw out a perfect pass in the other direction. The follow through was there, for there was nothing jerky about Tommy's passing.

Dai Davies, who has come from Warrington to Huddersfield in recent times, reminds me a lot of Tommy Grey. Davies has the same gliding movement in attack – he slips over the ground rather than runs on it – and he passes well, too. But Tommy was an artist where passing was concerned. He would go in between a couple of men who would hold him, and then he would lean forward and with a beautiful motion, sling the ball out easily and surely.

Rosenfeld was not merely a scoring machine as so many wingmen are in these days. He was a complete footballer, and he had the heart of a lion. I never saw a more dangerous wingman. When he came to us, he could not kick a ball – he was a running threequarter. It was, of course, necessary for him to learn to kick, for there are times when a wingman, to complete his attack, must be able to kick.

Rosenfeld's first efforts at kicking really were amusing. There were times when he actually kicked the ball back over his head. What did he do about it? He simply set out to learn to kick; took a ball out; and practiced and there came a time, as all know, when his short punt and fast follow up earned him many a try.

Tribute to Moorhouse

Moorhouse would have been a great wingman in any team. I know there were those who said that Stanley owed a lot to me. I know that Stanley was a brilliant footballer. He had a big match temperament, and I could always depend upon him. More than that, I could always tell to a few inches whether he could score and it was very seldom indeed that he let me down when I gave him a pass.

He had a kick through of his own that was just as effective as that developed by Rosenfeld, though it was of an entirely different kind. Moorhouse going at top speed could kick in his stride – the ball just left his hands for his feet and shot away in front but there was no slackening of Stanley's speed. He could kick-through on the ground for himself, or he could kick across for his forwards, and when he kicked across for his forwards it was rare indeed that he did not find them there waiting the move.

I remember well one try that Stanley got with his kick through. It was scored against the Australians at Fartown in 1911–12. The kick had, of course, been designed for his forwards; but, with that long raking stride of his he followed it up, regained possession of the ball near the posts and scored as he liked. And when he scored, he had a couple of our forwards with him. Had there been any need he could have passed to either of them and with the pass given his man a try.

That was one of the secrets of our great success in those happy days. Every man in the side knew his job and every man in the side was prepared to work to help another man to accomplish the job in front of the team. There was never any question of a man feeling, when he had done this or that, that his part in the move was finished. He was there to work for the team all the time and all the way.

Next, I shall have something to say about our forwards, about the power of Wrigley, about the skill of Tom Gleeson who replaced Wrigley and about the arrival of Johnny Rogers and the others.

7. Memorable try that astonished Wigan

The strength of our pack between 1911 and the outbreak of War – it was in season 1914–15, as I shall tell later, that we equalled Hunslet's Four Cup record – was that it contained weight, speed and skill. If circumstances arose that made it desirable that the forwards should have 'a bit of a do'... well, then they were perfectly capable of taking care of themselves. They never were simply a ball getting lot; they always were a fighting part of the team in every way.

But before I turn to the forwards, I must pay tribute to the part played by Edgar Wrigley in building that team. Wrigley was a centre of the big bustling type – the sort of centre Leeds, for instance, would give a lot of money for in these times. He took a lot of the weight off my shoulders in many matches because of his strength; but do not run away with the idea that he simply was a bustling centre, for that would be wrong.

There are several centres of the bustling sort in the game nowadays. The trouble with them however, is that they do not know what to do when they have done their bustling. Wrigley always did know what to do, for he was a footballer, as well as a man with the power to do the bustling.

And now for the forwards.

First of all, shall we say, there was Douglas Clark, the loose forward. His weight was true, his strength prodigious, and, with it all, he was fast. Clark's strength was so great that there were times when, I believe, he was afraid to use it on the field. Indeed, I know it is correct to say that only very occasionally did he go all out.

I used to hope that something would happen early in a match to get him going, there were times when I would 'kid' him to make him go a little more. He was, I firmly believe, afraid of his great strength.

Con Byrne, when he was with us, was a great asset. He was almost the ideal type of New Zealand forward and with him in the second row there was that great artist Ben Gronow. Ben played for Wales in the first international at Twickenham, and then he joined the Northern Union game. It was not long before we at Fartown realised something of the value there was in Ben's long pass from the ruck.

Gronow's great passes

What would clubs with fast backs give for a man of Ben's ability in these days, when there is the open play-the-ball rule? He would be worth scores of tries in a season to any club. Ben would be there when the ball came loose, and he would set out as though intending to pass to one wing. So far would he go and then he would stop, and, with unerring accuracy whirl a tremendously long pass to the other wing.

The defence, caught on the wrong foot, would be helpless. As long as I live, I shall remember Ben's great passes to his backs. There were times when he would hurl the ball half the width of the field and find his men almost as easily as though he were shooting with a rifle. There was a pass made at Sydney in 1920 – but that is a story I must tell later, for that was the game in which Harold Horder's body swerve made me wonder what I knew about football.

For the front row there were such men as John Willie Higson, who always packed on the field side, Sherwood, Wimpenny Brook, and Fred Longstaff, who, like quite a few other members of the side, was a really good goalkicker.

Brook was near the end of his career about this time – 1911–12 – but he still showed in his work evidence of the considerable speed he had possessed. Don't forget that he, a front row forward who always gave of his best in the pack, was an 11 seconds man. I have grateful memories of the interest Wimpenny showed in me when I, a lad from his own village, joined the side. He took me under his wing, and as long as he played with the side, he kept me under his wing. I know for certain that, in caring for me, he got himself sent off in one match, and I am almost certain that he got himself sent off in another match in "looking after t' lad from home."

Anyway, there you have an idea of the mettle and power and pace of the pack we had with us in those days. Byrne returned somewhat unexpectedly to Australia at the start of 1912–13, but we were admirably equipped with reserves and we thought this was to be our Four Cup season.

Shattered hopes

As a matter of fact, we went into January without being beaten in the league until we fell at Hull, but our Four Cup hopes were shattered at Craven Street, when Hull KR beat us in the first round of the competition by 9 points to 3. Hick, a very fast lad they had, got the try that settled the issue, for the score was 3–4 when he raced away with the ball.

Before that match with Hull KR we had one of our many memorable games with Wigan – a game we won in the last minute. That afternoon at Fartown, Wigan led by 10–3 at half-time, but we turned round to have the wind at our backs. Then, Wigan, contrary to custom, contended themselves with playing a purely defensive game.

We scored a try after 20 minutes of the half, to make the score 10–8; but, though we tried every move we knew we could not get those other points. There came a scrummage on the Wigan 25, and I shouted to Arthur Bennett, the trainer, asking him how long we had to go. He replied "Thee minutes".

Then I told Major Holland, the full-back, to be ready to make an extra threequarter, I told Douglas Clark that we must have the ball from the pack, and I told Tommy Grey and Jim Davies, the halves, that it was the last scrummage.

Now, that scrummage was placed about the 25 line nearer the terrace side than the centre of the field. I took up my position to the left of the scrum – on the short side – and opposite was Lance Todd, who had been on top of me throughout the second half. It was Todd's close watch that gave me the idea I was able to work when the forwards duly heeled. Tommy Grey flung out the pass, but instead of Jim Davies taking it, I stepped in to run with the ball diagonally to the right and open side of the scrummage. Straightaway, Lance Todd was cut out. He had advanced so far in his effort to watch me that he found himself on the wrong side of the scrummage.

Johnny Thomas had to come into me to make the tackle. Bert Jenkins, the other Wigan centre, had to take Jim Davies. Curwen, the wingman, had to challenge Wrigley, and there was Rosenfeld clear of all, save Sharrock, the Wigan full-back.

Rosenfeld did not know that Major Holland had taken up a position outside him, and, instead of drawing Sharrock and passing to Holland, he tried to beat Sharrock. He went down in a tackle.

When Rosenfeld and Sharrock got up to play-the-ball, I was there to support Rosenfeld, and Charlie Seeling, who had covered in defence like the grand loose forward he was, had support for Sharrock. Holland was a little to the right behind the play-the-ball.

Sharrock tried to clear with a fly-kick, but only half hit the ball, which shot into Major's hands and Major wasted no time in scoring the try that gave us a victory that sent scores of hats sailing into the air. The goal kick failed, the ball was kicked out from the centre and the last whistle sounded.

Gleeson's First Game

On the evening of that great victory, auburn haired Tom Gleeson arrived in Huddersfield from Australia, and straightaway the Fartown Committee found itself in a difficulty, for Gleeson quickly began to show form, and there we were with Wagstaff, Wrigley and Gleeson for the centre positions, and Rosenfeld, Moorhouse, Kitchin and Todd for the wing berths.

Gleeson's first game for Huddersfield was on the wing. Tom was a centre. He said so and said as well that he did not fancy 'relegation' to the wing. His Irish temper flared up and it looked like being a bit awkward, but I was able to get a word with him and smooth things out.

He went out to make himself at once a great favourite with the Fartown crowd. The match was with Dewsbury and very early on snow began to fall, much to the amazement of Tom, who had never seen any snow. He did not know what to make of it, and it looked as though the arrival of the snow was going to upset his game, but we had not been playing long before he got the ball between the halfway and the 25.

He set off as only he could do, and instead of sticking to his wing – he was opposite Billy Rhodes who had the proud record of not having had a try scored on his wing that season – he cut across the field, and running brilliantly, beat man after man to score at the other corner.

So, we carried on, always taking six three quarters with us – Todd played chiefly with the reserves –and ringing the changes on centres and wings. We secured that dashing forward Jack Chilcott, and with him in the pack we met the Hull KR side that had beaten us in the Yorkshire Cup and this time we put 30 points up against them.

Arrival of Johnny Rogers

In every way we were set nicely to retain the League Championship and to win for the first time the Northern Union Cup; but we had a sad blow in League match with Bramley at Fartown, on March 1 – Bramley again.

That was the game in which Johnny Rogers, who signed on the previous Thursday evening, played first in Huddersfield's colours; but Rogers was not eligible for the cup competition and it was only for the sake of giving him a run out in a comfortable match that he played that afternoon.

Beating Bramley by 73 points to 5 – we scored 17 tries – we made certain of the Yorkshire League Championship for that season. But we lost the services of Rosenfeld, who was sent off near the close, and Tommy Grey, who broke a small bone in his hand.

An extraordinary day was that. To start with, our spectators made a collection of between £20 and £30 to help Bramley along, and then Johnny Rogers, who had been obtained as an off-half, – he took Jim Davies's place in that game – had to move to scrum-half when Grey was hurt. I went off-half to him, and it was not long before we all realised that instead of having in Rogers a promising off-half, we had in him the makings of a brilliant scrum-half.

However, we were not able to use him in the cup competition, and so the following week when we went to St Helens in the first round of the Cup, we did not know what the team would be until half an hour before the kick off. The injury to Grey and the suspension of Rosenfeld for two matches had upset everything.

In the end, I played off-half to Jim Davies. Gleeson and Wrigley were the centres and Todd and Moorhouse the wings. I had had a little experience at off-half – Jim Davies and I would change places in a match if things were going really well – but Jim was not so happy at scrum-half, and in the second half, when we were against the wind he was penalised time and again for not getting the ball in straight. In desperation, he threw the ball to me asking me to see what I could do; but I fared no better for I was penalised first time.

A thrilling try

Anyway, we won the match comfortably enough and so we retained the same formation for the game with Batley at Mount Pleasant in the second round played the following Saturday. Victory was gained and we were able to field pretty well our full strength for the third round game with Wigan, when Jim Davies and Grey were half-backs again. Rosenfeld and Gleeson the wings and the pack was at its best.

The Central Park ground was not big enough for the crowd that hoped to see that classic cup tie and there were hundreds from Huddersfield among the thousands who were locked out. The big thrill of a great open game was the try scored by Tom Gleeson when he jumped clean over Sharrock's head to touch down at the corner.

There followed the semi-final with Wakefield Trinity at Halifax and the final with Warrington at Headingley – the final in which Skelhorne would have robbed us of the cup had he known what to do with the ball when he got it very near the end. But that is a story I shall tell next week.

8. Our first Northern Union Cup win

If Skelhorne, that grand Warrington forward, had not been so amazed when he got in the most unexpected fashion the gift of a try scoring opening in the closing minutes of the final at Headingley in 1913, Huddersfield's first success in the Northern Union Cup, as it was then, would have been delayed by a couple of seasons.

But Skelhorne was amazed – so amazed that he dealt with the ball for seconds – and we were saved by Tommy Gleeson shooting in from nowhere to make the Cup saving tackle. That season, we beat Wakefield Trinity in the semi-final at Halifax, a match distinguished by Jim Davies scoring the most impudent try I ever saw and Warrington rather surprisingly beat Dewsbury, the Cup holders in the other semi-final. So, instead of the anticipated Dewsbury–Huddersfield final it was an inter-county final that was staged at Headingley.

And Warrington, with their stern and hard forwards, gave us plenty to think about. They led 5–0 at half-time and it was not until well in the second half that we began to get any reward for all our passing efforts. Then Stanley Moorhouse scored three tries, and, with the game 9–5, everything seemed happy for us. Still, Warrington kept at it, and they had one particularly fierce attack on our lines. The dribble, in which Major Holland our full-back had a part, took the ball to the halfway line, and that seemed to be the end of it.

Gleeson to the Rescue

But Ben Jolley, the Warrington full-back, took the ball off the toes of our dribblers, and got in a kick towards our line. One of our men made an effort to field it, but did no more than touch it and so Skelhorne, a few yards from our line, was on side when this present from the gods fell into his hands

He had been left behind in the clearing dribble, and he was returning up the field when the ball flew straight to him. There was the way to a try as clear as could be for there was no Huddersfield man between him and the line. It looked like a five points try and it would have been a five points try had Skelhorne set off at once. But he was so astonished that he stood there with the ball unable to believe the piece of luck that had fallen to Warrington. When he did set off Tommy Gleeson, crossing from the other wing, was in pursuit and he found in the dying minutes of the game the pace with which to catch Skelhorne. The tackle was made no more than three yards from the line.

So, the Northern Union Cup went to Fartown for the first time, but the margin of four points was nothing like sufficient for many of our supporters, who in those days had developed the habit of giving many points start. We had won the Cup without playing a single tie at Fartown. We had realised a great ambition, and I can tell you that we were very pleased about it all.

Jim Davies and I were especially pleased, and, after a bit of food at The George, in Huddersfield, a dinner at which many nice things were said about the team, we set off for a walk in town. What a shock there was for us. Almost everybody we met asked us why we had won by no more than four points, and in the end, we fled to a quiet spot where we could have a drink and reassure ourselves that we really had won the Cup.

It puzzled and worried Jim no end, and I remember that just about the last thing he said that night when he went home with me, was: "Tell me, Harold, have we won this – Cup or have we lost it".

An impudent try

There will be many who will remember the impudent try Jim scored in the semi-final with Wakefield at Halifax. It was a try which set a wildly-enthusiastic crowd rocking with laughter, when, really there ought to have been tremendous cheering for a wonderful piece of football. For it was wonderful football and that despite its impudence.

Jim took the half somewhere near the halfway line, and if he gave the dummy once he gave it 10 times before he put the ball down behind the posts. I know because I was alongside him all the time, waiting for the pass that would send me over. Jim would hold the ball out as though intending to pass to me, and I would prepare for the burst, only to find that Jim had slipped past another man. Three or four times the opening was made but, still Jim went on, serving out dummies with the greatest of ease, until, finally, he handed out the best of them all.

This time, I felt certain that he had passed the ball, and I went for the line only to find when I got there that Jim had kept the ball and scored himself. I could have sworn that I had the ball when I went over the line.

The season ended with us beating Wigan in the Final for the Northern Rugby League Championship, and there we were with three cups again. In that season of 1912–13 in which we lost four league matches – we were beaten by Hull, Wigan, Oldham and York – we won the Yorkshire League, the Northern Union Cup and the Northern Rugby League Championship.

The only other defeat we sustained that season came in the first round of the Yorkshire Cup when we went down before Hull Kingston Rovers. Johnny Rogers had joined us on March 1 – Aaron Lee, the hooker from Leigh, was another of our acquisitions that season – and he was very upset at not being called upon to take his place in the side in the League Championship Final, and he talked about returning to his home in Wales. However, I was able to point out to him the big chance there was for him at Fartown. He saw it and stayed and, in the season of 1913–14 he was, as all know, a most valuable member of the side.

Tribute to Johnny Rogers

When Johnny joined us, he looked a boy but he was a footballer all the time and all the way. I have told how he made his first appearance at off-half in the match with Bramley, in which Tommy Grey, the scrum half, was injured and how Johnny went to scrum-half to show at once that it was his best position.

Jim Davies, who was rested that day, watched the game from the side and when it was all over, and Johnny had established himself immediately as a Fartown favourite, I said to Jim: "How do you like the little lad?"

Now Jim, as straightforward a fellow as ever I knew, always said what he thought. His reply was "He's no good to me. How the ---- can I expect to keep up with him?" But Jim did keep up with him and as Johnny stepped into the shoes of Tommy Grey another great half-back partnership blossomed.

Johnny Rogers was the best scrum half I played with – more than that, he was the best scrum-half I ever saw.

He knew the game from A to Z, his hands were sure and his passes accurate, he varied his play in brilliant fashion and, most important of all, he was wonderfully fast into action. Those who saw Rogers break away from the scrummage when he was at his best will understand just what I mean. He got the ball and he was away with it, and that was all there was about it.

For 60 yards or so Johnny Rogers in those days was the fastest man in the game. Billy Batten always said to me: "Harold, you cannot do anything with Johnny, He may break away any time and if he does … Well, what chance have we then."

Anyway, there we were at the beginning of 1913–14 satisfied that this was to be our four cups season. We began by capturing the Yorkshire Cup we had lost in the previous season, but the final was one in which I did not play.

Chosen for Australia

During the week before that cup final with Bradford Northern at Halifax, I was troubled ever so much with what I thought were indigestion pains. I was compelled to see a doctor. The doctor without delay took me to Leeds to see Sir Berkeley Moynihan and at that interview, I was told that I must not think about playing in the final. My instructions were to prepare myself for a course of treatment in a nursing home. For years I had been troubled with this knifelike pain in the stomach. I used to carry arrowroot biscuits about with me and nibble them before a game; I found that they eased the pain.

In the nursing home they put me on a diet which consisted chiefly of milk, weak tea and custards, and when I left the home on January 1, I weighed 10 stones 10 pounds instead of 12 stones 4 pounds. I was concerned about it, for I was desperately anxious to get a place in the Rugby League team for Australia that summer. Illness had cost me a place in the 1910 side and it looked as though illness was to rob me of a place in the 1914 side.

However, I got going all right, and, after captaining England against Wales at St Helens, I was given my place in the team for Australia. After that international game at St Helens the first five men were selected for Australia and three of them, Longstaff, Clark and myself, were from Huddersfield.

Huddersfield played good football through that season, and we held the Yorkshire League Championship, but to our amazement we saw both the Northern Union Cup and the Northern Rugby League Championship leave us. Hull beat us 9–3 in the semi-final for the Cup at Headingley – they had a back division composed of Rogers, Francis, Harrison, Batten, Gilbert, Devereux and Anderson – and there were those who said we lost the match because the six Huddersfield men selected for the tour – Clark, Chilcott, Longstaff, Rogers, Moorhouse and myself – were thinking more about the Australian trip than anything else. The facts are that Hull had a powerful side in those days, that nothing went right for us that afternoon, and that they scored three goals and one try to one try.

Rosenfeld record

But there was a worse blow to follow. The following week Salford beat us 5–3 in the Final for the League, when the odds were reckoned to be a 100 to one on us.

Salford themselves did not think they had a chance. They had scrambled into the 'First Four' and then they had somewhat flukily beaten Wigan in the semi-finals. Everything happened the wrong way for us that afternoon. Salford got a try at the corner and kicked the goal. We scored near the posts and missed the goal. The ball was knocked on when the way to the line was clear, there were forward passes when the defence had been well beaten, and so in just about every way we thoroughly disappointed the 12,000 spectators who had gathered for the game. The attendance was the smallest at any League Final for years – people had not bothered to go because they said it would not be a match.

The outstanding feature that season was the creation by Rosenfeld of his scoring record of 80 tries – a record that many never be beaten – and there were, of course, the two Wigan matches and the Halifax match at Thrum Hall in the Yorkshire Cup. We beat Halifax by 39–0 and that was the match in which Tommy Gleeson scored four tries. It was also the match before which Joe Riley who had been to Australia with Jim Davies in 1910 and knew all about Jim's ability to sell the dummy, told the Halifax players that they must refuse to take it. They must make, he said, a point of taking Davies no matter what happened.

The point of the story is that Joe Riley was without question one of the best tacklers in the League in those days. Remembering that, one gets an idea of the great skill Davies displayed when he really set out to give the dummy to anyone.

In the games with Wigan that season there was some astonishing scoring. We were beaten 35–3 at Central Park and we won the return game at Fartown by 46–10.

9. 'Four Cups' season at Fartown

Huddersfield's league matches with Wigan in 1913–14 produced the best football and the most astonishing results. In November, we went to Wigan after we had run up a big score against Halifax in the Yorkshire Cup competition, and we were beaten by 35 points to 3. Yet no one could say that there was anything like 30 points between the sides in this game, in which play flashed from end to end at a bewildering pace.

Each side stood back to attack, and each side attacked, but whereas Wigan kept notching points with tries at the corners, we kept just missing them, and Francis, the New Zealand forward – he had been to England with the 1911 Australians – kicked goal after goal from the touchline. We had just as much of the attack as Wigan, and we were just as clever in attack as they were, until it came to the all-important matter of getting points.

No team tried harder than we did that day but the points simply would not come. That was the first match in which I played against Gwyn Thomas. He tackled me with unfailing regularity and in one way and another game me as stern a gruelling as any centre threequarter – he played centre three-quarter that day – had done for years

From South Wales

Of course, we waited for the return game at Fartown in February and so did many others. That day, they ran a special train from South Wales to Huddersfield, among the visitors from the Principality being the late Keir Hardie. Thirteen of the 26 men engaged in that match were Welshmen, as you will see from the teams [Welsh players in capitals]:

Huddersfield: Holland, Rosenfeld, Gleeson, Wagstaff, Moorhouse ROGERS, DAVIES, JONES, Lee, Longstaff, GRONOW, CHILCOTT, Clarke.
Wigan: THOMAS (GWYN), BRADLEY, JENKINS, CURRAN, Curwen, OWENS, THOMAS (JOHNNY) COLDRICK Silcock, HAYWARD, Francis, Ramsdale, Seeling. [In fact, Bradley had played rugby union for Pontypool, but was English and Curran was a New Zealander.]

We took adequate revenge, scoring 46–10. Just as everything had gone in favour of Wigan at Wigan, everything went for us that February afternoon at Fartown. Wigan played good football, but the points they sought did not come, while we could do nothing wrong. Our forwards, I always thought, played one of their very best games that day. Their passing rushes and their dribbling attacks were simply marvellous.

At the end of the season there was the Australian tour on which I went along with Clark, Longstaff, Rogers, Moorhouse, and Chilcott of Huddersfield. There were many who said that the League might have sent the entire Huddersfield team of those days on that tour, and there were many who thought that Jim Davies was almost certain to go with us. Jim thought he had a big chance, and his belief was increased by the fact that he played very fine football in matches with the men who were thought to be his chief rivals for the off-half position.

... John James O'Hara

Ganley (Leeds), Thomas (Wigan) and Prosser (Halifax) were all in the running; but Jim outplayed them man by man. And then came the shock when the team was announced, Prosser (Halifax) and O'Garra (Widnes) were the off-halves

I shall never forget the morning the team for Australia was announced. Jim turned up at Fartown for practice, but he was so surprised at the selection of the Widnes man that he was almost speechless. He marched into the dressing room, and implored someone to tell him who the so-and-so this Mister O'Garra was. Now, that year, there was a popular song that had to do with the whereabouts of a Mister John James O'Hara: "Has anyone seen John James O'Hara playing on his trombone?" So, when Jim had finished his little piece, we all sang softly to him about John James O'Hara.

To complete the story – the song stayed with the team for the remainder of the season – I must say that a few weeks later we met Widnes, and that afternoon O'Garra played very fine football against Jim. It was when we were on the boat from New Zealand to Australia that we heard news of the outbreak of the war between England and Germany, and when we reached Australia, Jarman, Roman and

Robinson, members of that Tour team, had to report to the military authorities, for they were reservists. They were allowed to travel home with us, through the waters in which the Emden was operating, but these were matters about which I will tell in another article.

Two defeats only

We got back to Huddersfield late in September, and then I believe Huddersfield had lost one of the four matches in which they had played. We went into the side for the game at Barrow – we were not fit – and there we were beaten. But that was the last defeat we suffered that season. We played through six and a half months of football without defeat. We took the Yorkshire Cup and the Yorkshire League, and at the end of the season we captured the League Championship and the Rugby League Cup, and so completed our ambition of equalling Hunslet's Four Cups feat.

There is not a lot to tell about that season. We were held to a division of points at Leeds, and at the Craven Street Ground of the Hull Kingston Rovers club, but for the rest it was a long triumphant march. At the start of the season, Bob Habron was the off-half in place of Jim Davies, who as the end of the previous season had returned to Wales and who enlisted at the start of the War. As a youngster, Jim had served in the South African War.

Wrigley had gone to Hunslet, transferred there in July 1914, and from Hunslet we had secured another fine forward in Herbert Banks. After the Yorkshire Cup Final, in which we beat Hull and so obtained revenge for the defeat sustained in the R.L. Cup Final of the previous season, we secured the transfer of Bert Ganley from Leeds, and he was fast and clever enough to be able to strike a partnership with Johnny Rogers.

Chilcott had left Huddersfield to play with Leeds, and he was in the Leeds side which met us at Wakefield in the final for the League Championship. That season, we headed the Northern Rugby League again, Wigan were second, Leeds third and Hull fourth. Leeds, who had found brilliant end-of-season form gave Wigan a rare thrashing in the semi-final, and they turned up at Wakefield confident that they could put an end to our long run of success.

The forwards did it

Their followers had any amount of confidence, too, and we knew that we were 'up against it'. For in their back division they had such men as Lewis, the full-back, Campbell and Willie Davies, the centres, and they had a tremendously fast pack of forwards. They banked entirely on their speed. When we were in the dressing room preparing for the match, we talked over our prospects. We decided that our forwards should keep the ball until I told Clark that the backs wanted it. The game had not gone many minutes when we scrummaged on the Leeds '25'. Our forwards heeled the ball and straightaway four of the Leeds forwards tore away from the pack in the expectation that the ball would be sent out to the Huddersfield backs.

But our forwards held it, took it with them to the Leeds line, and there Douglas Clark picked up the ball to score a try as he liked. Gronow kicked the goal. Inside five minutes, the move had been repeated, the only difference being that Gronow got the try this time. So, Leeds were 10 points down in eight minutes, and our backs had not handled the ball.

Their forwards were rushing about the field looking for someone to tackle and so I told Clark to let us have the ball the next time his forwards got it. Rogers sent on to Ganley, and Ganley let me have the ball. Again, the Leeds forwards went dashing across the field to cover the wingman, and so they left me an avenue as wide as could be.

I went up to Lewis, the Leeds full-back, and I was just preparing to make an effort to beat him when I heard a voice alongside me shouting: "Suit – Suit – Suit". I turned round and popped the ball into the hands of Fred Longstaff, and he scored under the posts for Gronow to kick another goal. There was nothing to it after that, Leeds were demoralised, and the only reply they had to our 31 points was a goal finely dropped by Lewis. There was the evidence of our all-round strength. Our forwards paved the way with tactics the other side never expected them to use.

Fred Longstaff's Suit

And now a word of explanation about the cry Longstaff made when he asked for the pass which enabled him to score the third try.

The previous night, Fred and I were walking along Huddersfield's main street when we met a tailor, who promised me the best suit he had in the shop if we beat Leeds. Fred said "You fellows always think about the backs and never about the forwards. What do I get if we win?" Thereupon the tailor said that Fred could also have a suit if he scored a try. Hence Fred's frantic shout of "Suit – Suit –Suit" when he found himself alongside me and the way to the line open. Fred had something to say the following week too when we played St Helens in the Cup Final at Oldham. In that match, our followers were giving ever so many points start, and at half time one of our keenest followers sent word to me that if we won by 30 points there was half-a-sovereign for every member of the side.

Huddersfield RLFC 1914–15: Players: Back: A. Lee, JW Higson, H. Banks, E. Jones, E. Heyes, F. Longstaff, D. Clark, A. Swinden; middle: R. Habron, M. Holland, S. Moorhouse, H. Wagstaff (capt.), T. Gleeson, G. Todd, B. Gronow; front: WH. Ganley, A. Rosenfeld, J. Rogers. Trophies: Yorkshire League, Northern Rugby League, Challenge Cup, Yorkshire Cup. (Courtesy Robert Gate)

Harold Wagstaff and Huddersfield RLFC trainer Arthur Bennett and the 'Four Cups' won in 1914–15. (Courtesy Robert Gate)

Now half-a-sovereign was half-a-sovereign in those times, and I passed the message round. We were well away with the game by then, but in the second half I began to feel ever so tired. The truth was that I had played three hard seasons in a row, two in England and one in Australia and I was a bit leg weary. Anyway, it happened that when I was favourably placed twice in the early minutes of the second half, I lost the ball. Fred saw this, and before long he was on my track.

"If you don't want that ten bob," he yelled, "there's a few of us that can do with it." He got his half sovereign all right. We won by five goals, nine tries (37 points) to one try (3 points), and everybody was satisfied.

Ben kicks goals

That was the season in which we scored 1,222 points to 275 and that was the season in which Ben Gronow kicked 140 goals. As a matter of fact, Ben broke Carmichael's goalkicking record of 138 with the fourth goal he kicked in the final with St Helens at Oldham.

And yet, you know, Ben only became our goalkicker accidentally. It was at Bramley in the November of 1914 – yes, Bramley again – that Major Holland, troubled with a strained thigh, asked me to give the goalkicking job to someone else. It was a shocking day, wet and windy, and the ground was a patch of mud, but Ben, who took Major's goal kicking place kicked nine goals in nine shots. He landed them from all over the place, and after that we were bound to keep him at work.

140 goals, or 150 with the 10 he kicked in a friendly match at Swinton at the end of the season, between December and May represented a magnificent piece of work. With that Four Cups season, competitive rugby league football finished until after the War. Next week I will tell of the revival of the side after the War, and of the hard luck we had in not repeating the Four Cups feat in 1919–20.

10. Men who won the four cups

In season 1914–15, when we won the four cups, the side generally was: Holland, Rosenfeld, Gleeson, Wagstaff, Moorhouse, Ganley, Rogers, Longstaff, Lee, Higson, Gronow, Banks Clark; but the importance of the parts played by such men as Habron, Swinden and Todd must not be overlooked.

They were first-class men who had to be content to be on reserve often, yet they were so good that any other club in the league would have been glad to pay a substantial transfer fee for any one of them.

Todd, in fact, was the fourth highest try scorer that season. Rosenfeld got 55, Moorhouse 48, I had 34, Todd 33, Gleeson 27, Rogers 26 and Ganley 17. And when we played a friendly match at Swinton at the end of that season – a match which realised its financial object and enabled Swinton to clear off an old-standing debt – we kept on the scoring track.

Swinton take a lesson

The most important feature of that Swinton friendly, however, was the impression made by the fast open football. The Swinton officials thereupon declared that, when serious football was resumed after the War, they would insist upon their men working on open lines, and, as everyone knows, they did. They were so successful, in fact, that in 1928 they emulated our four cups feat.

Often I have been asked to speculate on the work that would have been accomplished by that 1914–15 Huddersfield team had it not been for the War. My reply has always been the same.

Take the ages of the men in the side in 1915. I was 23, Holland was 26, Rosenfeld 27, Gleeson 25, Moorhouse 23, Rogers 22, Ganley 26, Clark 23, Gronow 25, Banks 25, Higson 27, Longstaff 26, Lee 28, Todd 22 and Habron 23.

The side was young enough to thrive, and the fact is that in 1919–20 the team, with one or two changes, went through to take three of the four cups, and only lost the fourth because five of its members, Gwyn Thomas, Clark, Gronow, Rogers and myself, had to miss the final because of the claims of the 1920 tour team.

The story of post-war football at Huddersfield starts with the side's success in the Yorkshire Cup competition, which was run in the early months of 1919. When the War finished, I was in Egypt, Rogers was in hospital – he had been gassed – and Rosenfeld was in Mesopotamia.

I mention the three of us because, in the early months of 1919 we found ourselves in Royd's Hall Hospital, Huddersfield, and it was from Royd's Hall Hospital that we, in hospital blue, used to sneak out to do our training at Fartown and to play in cup matches.

From hospital to cup tie

I remember the day we played Hull Kingston Rovers at Hull in the Cup. We had a very early breakfast, and we slipped quietly out of hospital to catch the train to Hull.

I was not fit to play, but Rosenfeld, who had a medical board the previous week, and Rogers, who was waiting for a medical board, played under the names of Jones and Brown, and covered themselves in glory. We beat Dewsbury in the final, and the following season when Northern Rugby League football started again, we kept the Yorkshire Cup by beating Leeds in the final at Halifax.

By that time, we had secured Gwyn Thomas from Wigan, and we had had to replace such men as Longstaff – Fred was killed in the War – Aaron Lee, the hooker, who had settled in America, Jim Davies who had remained in Wales, and Banks who had smashed his ankle while at work in the pit, and who had, consequently, to retire from the game.

Arthur Sherwood had thrown in his lot with us, and we got such forwards as Taylor and Fenwick. With Ganley returning to his home in Leigh in the December of that year, we were content to rely upon Habron as the off-half. Habron played very fine football that day we beat Leeds at Halifax; but my chief memory of the game in which we scored 24 points to 5, concerns a tackle made on me by Jim Bacon.

I had heard about Jim, and the try he had scored to beat the New Zealand Trench team down in Wales; but I had never seen him before that afternoon. Anyway, I soon felt his power. I took a pass and went sailing away comfortably, I thought, for a try, when this young Welsh wing-threequarter came into me with a head-on tackle.

I was taken to the touch-line, and as the tackle had hit me right in the weak spot in my stomach, I thought frankly that I was done for. After five minutes or so I was able to return with, I may say, a great respect for the strength of Bacon, who told me after the match that he thought he had broken his neck in the tackle. There were few men in the game able to tackle me in such a fashion in those times.

We had another great game with Wigan that season. They beat us 12–8, and Danny Hurcombe, who dropped a goal from halfway, had so fine a match that, chiefly on the strength of his work that afternoon, he was given a place in the Australian tour team.

Historic Bramley victory

It was in that season that Bramley – again – gained their historic victory over us. The Fartown Committee rested three of us that afternoon in preparation for the semi-final with Oldham the following week, and Bramley, with a flying start went on to reveal form that would have beaten most sides.

I recollect well enough being on the stand and I remember well enough the amount of chaff I had to stand. But there was no questioning the merit of the football played by Bramley that day. They earned every point of their victory.

Then came the cup semi-final with Oldham, and we were in a predicament, for Stanley Moorhouse was not fit to play, and with Gleeson on the injured list, we were short of a threequarter back.

In the second team there was a youngster named Pogson, who had some experience of Army football. He was a strong, straight runner, and he was always ready to have a go.

I said that he would do for me, and so, in the circumstances, the committee decided to give him a trial. So, we turned out with a back division in which Gwyn Thomas and I were centres in front of Major Holland, recalled to the full-back position. Pogson and Rosenfeld were the wings, and Habron and Rogers the half-backs.

After about a quarter of an hour, I got a chance of letting Pogson have the ball, and he went away like the good 'un he was, to finish with a try under the posts. He played grand football for the remainder of the game, and he played just as well in the final for the Cup when we met Wigan at Headingley.

Wigan got a try early on for obstruction, but at half-time we led 10–5. They were finely served in that grand game by Jerram, one of their halves, and Shaw, their loose-forward; but Pogson came into his own in the last 20 minutes, and we won comfortably enough, 21–10.

We had then three of the four cups, and we seemed to have in Pogson the makings of a great international wing threequarter. But just as Pogson, owing to injury, was to fall away, so we were to fail in our four cups ambition.

We had to play Hull in the final for the League, and the team had to turn out without those of us chosen to go to Australia and without Moorhouse, who was still injured. Yet the youngsters who took our places fought so well that they were only beaten in the last few minutes by a try scored by Billy Batten.

My benefit game

Before that final, Gwyn Thomas, J. Rogers, D. Clark, Ben Gronow and myself sailed for Australia, and before we sailed, I, to celebrate my benefit, gave a little dinner to the members of the Huddersfield side. We had the Huddersfield Town men as our guests.

Everything pointed to that being a record year for sport in Huddersfield, for Town, who had secured promotion, were in the final for the FA Cup, and we looked like accomplishing the four cups feat again. But Town went down to Aston Villa on the Chelsea ground, and we, as I have said, just failed, with a sadly weakened team, to beat a full-strength Hull side.

I took the Rochdale Hornets league match at Fartown as my benefit game, chiefly because my mother had come from Rochdale, and though the day – 17 January 1920 – was a deplorable one, with rain pouring down from the first thing in the morning until just before the kick-off, there were over 18,000 spectators at Fartown. That was one of the biggest tributes paid to me, and I always recall with pride and pleasure the way in which Huddersfield people, and quite a few people from outside Huddersfield, made my benefit a success. There was £980 for me when everything was reckoned.

On that 1920 Australian tour, Johnny Rogers had his leg broken, and he was carried off the boat when it docked in London. Gwyn Thomas, Clark, Gronow and I travelled overland from Marseille in order to be able to play with Huddersfield in the first round of the Yorkshire Cup, but our rush was of no avail, for we were beaten by Dewsbury at Crown Flatt after a draw at Fartown.

"On the slide"

The greatest Huddersfield team had ridden on the crest of the wave long enough. The slide down the slope – the gradual slide – began. Of the three trophies won in 1919–20, the only one we retained was the Yorkshire League Championship, though we were a little unfortunate, I always thought, to be beaten in the semi-final of the Northern Union Cup by Halifax, who fell heavily in the final with Leigh.

In those days, the Huddersfield Committee made it a custom to rest two or three men before a big game. I never thoroughly agreed with the policy, arguing that, frequently, it threw extra work on the first team men left in the side. Anyway, Clark, myself and Rosenfeld stood out of the side against Bradford, and in making a big effort in that game, Rogers damaged his ankle, and was unable to play in the semi-final.

About that time, such men as Stamper and Stanley Williams, a clever and fast footballer, arrived at Fartown, and the following season we got men such as Davidge, Peter Reid, and, later on, Watts and McTighe. They all looked likely recruits; but somehow or other the old standard could not be maintained. The manoeuvring ability left the side; the tries did not come as easily as in the days gone by.

A game we had with Wakefield Trinity about that time stands clear in the memory. Habron, who dropped a goal in the first half, and Charlie Pollard, were in the Trinity side. We hammered their line for 20 minutes at one spell, but their tackling was magnificent. I don't think I can recall a game in which the tackling all the way round was as heroic or hard as in that match at Belle Vue.

Early in 1921–22, there was evidence for all of the nature of our decline, and that despite the acquisition of new and likely men.

We played the Australian tourists at Fartown and they ran away with us. Before that, we had always played the best of football against touring teams; but this day we were no match for Horder and the other men wearing the Kangaroos' jersey. Horder's try which took him almost the length of the field, is talked about in Huddersfield to this day.

There was a bit of a revival in 1922–23, when the half-back partnership of Jimmy May ad Stanley Williams counted for much, but we fell before Hull Kingston Rovers in the League Championship Final, and we were beaten by Leeds in the third round of the Cup.

A Kibbler story

That was the first cup match in which Joe Thompson played against us, and it was the first cup victory Leeds had secured over us for many a year. That was the match, too, in which Kibbler, the Leeds forward, took the ball out of my hands, to score a try near the posts. I got the ball about the '25' line, and dodging this way and that, tried to find a clearing opening. I 'offered' the ball here and there; but could not get away with it, and in the end, Kibbler apparently thought I was offering the ball to him. Anyway, he walked in to take it, and that was all there was about it.

In the second round game with Rochdale, I had curiously enough, helped myself to a try-scoring opening in precisely the same fashion. They say that the good man ought never to give anything away, and that he ought never to take the dummy; but I say that the cleverest man often gives things away, and is just as likely to take the dummy as anyone.

That third round cup game with Leeds marked the beginning of the end of my football career. After the match, I went into hospital for the duodenal ulcer operation that I had put off for so many years, and when I returned to play, I knew that the end of my long and happy playing connection with the game was in sight.

Next week I will tell of my closing games, and look back on my experience as a rugby union man in war-time football.

11. Some pleasant war-time contacts

At the start of the season 1923–24, when I was 32 years old, I was able to get into action at once. The duodenal ulcer operation – a job in which there was 14 stitches – compelled me to wear a specially made protective corset, and I spent a long time training in this before I was really comfortable.

However, it gave me the feeling of security I sought, and in the first match of that season – it was played at Bramley – I was able to find form to satisfy myself that I still had a bit of football left in me. But the stiff supports of the corset took away from the power to make the body swerve that had helped me so much and when I played against Hunslet at Huddersfield, somewhere about the middle of November, I decided that the time had come to try to go through a game without the protection of the corset. That day 'Dolly' Dawson was playing in the Hunslet three-quarter line, and there came a time when, just as I was preparing to pass to my wing man, he came into me with one of his very best tackles. His shoulder caught me right on the operation spot and I went down – clean out. They carried me to the touch line and there, when Clayton, the trainer, found that I had gone on to the field without my 'armour' he played the deuce. He sent to the dressing room for it, I put it on there and then, and I never played without it afterwards.

Missing the trophies

That season, Huddersfield played useful football without taking any trophies. We were beaten by Hull in the Yorkshire Cup final at Headingley, and we ran into the semi-final of the Rugby League Cup only to be beaten by Oldham at Halifax.

Oldham had such men as Hilton, Sloman, Knapman and Rix in their ranks in those days – they had a grand pack – and of our old side we had Clark, Gronow, Rogers and myself. But we reckoned up the Oldham side, and we prepared a plan of campaign and I am still convinced that the plan would have taken us to victory had it been adhered to.

Up to the last eight minutes we were leading 5–3. Rogers scored our try – I went out to the wing as though intending to past the ball to Ted Fisher and then, when I had taken the defence with me, I turned round and found as arranged that Johnny was there to take the ball and score. Not a hand was put on him as he went to the line. In the second half we were all over Oldham until, eight minutes from time Joe Oliver, our full-back, put in a little short kick in reply to a clearing kick by Knapman. Oliver hoped to be able to get the ball on the bounce, but Albert Brough, that very fast Oldham forward, was there before him. He took it and went away for the vital try. The try scored afterwards by Hilton did not matter, for the game which ought to have been won had been lost then.

Players' Thursday meeting

That was my last Cup semi-final, and I can tell you now that we started with the belief that we could win it. We made our plans and our preparations at the players' meeting at Fartown on the previous Thursday night, and when I look back and think of them the more I realised how important and valuable those meeting were.

Every man on the first team sheet for the following Saturday had to attend Fartown for this Thursday night meeting. Most of the men did their training during the afternoon, but none was allowed, unless he obtained special permission from the committee, to miss the meeting. And it was a meeting that was attended only by the players and the trainer. When there was a big match in prospect a committee man attended to have a little talk with us; but the discussion generally concerned only the men who were engaged for the following Saturday.

We always started in the same way – with a talk about the previous Saturday's game. Then I would ask anyone who had any idea about it to say what they had to say and when we had dealt with that business, we turned to the question of tactics for the following Saturday. If, say, for argument's sake, there had been a fault in the scrummaging the previous week the forwards would thrash that business out, and, as likely as not, get down in a pack to try and discover means of making things better.

The meetings had much to do with the creation of the team spirit that counted for everything when we were at our best, and I am perfectly certain that matches which might have been lost were won because of those Thursday evening talks.

Pointing out mistakes

When I was captain of Huddersfield and except for one break I captained Huddersfield from the end of 1910–11 until I retired – I always made it a rule to tell a man on the field when I thought he had made a mistake. Occasionally there were those who did not like this, and one man went to the committee with a complaint. My reply was that it was essential to tell a man of a mistake on the field in the hope of being able to prevent him from duplicating that mistake before the final whistle sounded.

My last season was 1924–25, and my last match with Huddersfield was played against Oldham on 29 March 1925. I had felt throughout the season, though never definitely worried, that the end was near. At Fartown, there were those who had different ideas, and Mr John Clifford who had signed me on so many years before, thought I should be able to serve Huddersfield well as a full-back for a year or two.

Anyway, I agreed to have a trial at full-back in this match with Oldham, but in it I damaged my ankle and that was the end of it all. I had moved from Huddersfield to Halifax in those days, and as Huddersfield were playing at Halifax in a charity match at the end of the season, I was pressed on both sides to make an effort to return for that one game.

I decided to give myself a try out first and on Easter Tuesday I played against Keighley 'A' for the Huddersfield 'A' team. That was the only occasion on which I played with the Huddersfield second team.

Except for the illness and injury, I was never off the Huddersfield first team sheet in the whole of my connection with the club.

Huddersfield's record

I scored 14 goals – most of them in my first season, when I got more goals than tries – and 185 tries for Huddersfield. In the time I was with them Huddersfield won the Yorkshire Cup six times and were runners up twice; they won the Yorkshire League five times and were runners up twice, they won the Northern Rugby League Championship three times, and were runners up thrice, and they won the Rugby League Cup three times.

I played my last game for Yorkshire in 1923–24, when Billy Batten and I were recalled to play centre against Lancashire, in a match in which we were beaten by a try scored by Crooks, the St Helens full-back, in the last minute and before I turn to my recollections of war-time football, I must tell one story of 1924–25 season.

In those days, I had as my centre colleague at Fartown a very likely player named McTighe who was ever so fond of 'floating the dummy'. Often, I had had to ask McTighe to cut the 'dummy', but that afternoon when we turned round at Batley no more than three points to the good, I called McTighe over and told him that he could try the "dummy" as much as he wanted. "As soon as I am first centre," I said to him, "I will draw Harry Rees, and you can see what you can do with your "dummy."

Right enough the chance came. I brought Harry Rees into me, and sent the ball out to McTighe and away he went. He served a dummy which sent Cyril Stacey away after the wing man, and McTighe went sailing over for a try. But, as soon as he put the ball down, he turned round and rushed 25 or 30 yards up the field to me seized my hand and yelled with joy "according to plan."

My first rugby union game

It was in 1915–16 that I played my first rugby union game. Mr RF Oakes, the secretary of the Yorkshire Rugby Union picked a side to play the Anzacs, who had just returned from Gallipoli and I, along with several other rugby league men, was asked to play with Mr Oakes's side. The game was for charity, and as the Rugby Union ban on rugby league players was lifted during the war, there was nothing to stop rugby league men playing rugby union football.

The game was played on the Leeds club's ground at Headingley. I had W.A. Davies, the Leeds centre, as my partner and at off-half there was Eddie Myers who that day showed promise of the form that was to make him one of England's greatest post-war internationals. In the Anzacs side there were Tom Gleeson and Devereux of Hull.

We had Johnny Rogers at scrum half, Clark and Gronow were in the forwards with such Yorkshire rugby union players as Frank Trenham, H.J. White of Headingley and Mason of Northumberland, the full-back. The match was refereed by Mr Arthur Yeadon, who now is the hon. Treasurer of the Headingley rugby union club.

It was the first of many fine rugby union games in which I played. I had only seen one rugby union match before that in which I played at Headingley – that was in Australia in 1914 – and I remember very well what a shock I had when I was penalised for not letting the ball go when tackled.

Another memory of that grand game has to do with a ginger head forward in the Australian side who found at half time that his boots were not comfortable. He took them off and played without them for the remainder of the game, and more than that he had several shots at goal without boots. After that, I played in several charity games with Mr Oakes's team. There was a game at Hartlepools on 29 April 1916 when I had Stanley Cook, of Gloucester, a fine player, as my centre partner.

Cook and I each relied on a fair amount of body action when making a run, and somehow or other we did not strike a partnership at once and the crowd began to ask us to do something. There came a scrum inside our opponents' half and Frank Trenham, our hooker, saw to it that we got the ball. Johnny Rogers, the half-back, let me have it on the burst and I went sailing through for a try that put me right with the Hartlepools crowd.

Billy Trew

Then there was a game on the Anfield ground, at Liverpool, in May 1916 where we beat a Welsh rugby union side by 5–3. That day I saw Billy Trew for the first and only time, and, though Billy Trew was getting on in years and though he played wing three-quarter, I had an opportunity that afternoon of understanding why it was that Jim Davies always said that Billy Trew was the best footballer he had ever seen.

Andrew Hamilton was the scrum-half that afternoon, and Johnny Rogers was the off-half in our team. They were pleasant experiences. The football was good and there were many friends to be made. Friendships were created then which still exist. When my son was born in 1917, I was happy at the request of Mr 'Bob' Oakes, to give him 'Bob' as a name, and when I had my benefit at Fartown in 1920 there was a gathering there that day of between 20 and 30 Yorkshire rugby union stalwarts who came over in a party to encourage me.

In 1916 I went into the Army and there I became a member of the Grove Park ASC team which was only beaten once. Of the men in that side and of some of my test match and international match experiences I will tell next week

12. All-star Grove Park team
Rugby league football under rugby union rules

In 1916 I was serving along with Gronow and Clark in the Army Service Corps at Grove Park. In the season that ended in 1916, Gronow and Clark had played a little rugby down there and in the season that started in the September of 1916, I found myself the member of a rugby union team again.

Major Stanley, who had been a member of the Rugby Union Selection Committee, and who takes, as he has done for years, a team to give Oxford University their final trial every season, was in charge of the Convoy Staff at Grove Park and it was to this staff that I was attached. I was a motor driver before I joined the Army and Gronow and Clark who were with me in one hut, used to drive heavy Lorries in convoy from Grove Park to such places as Avonmouth, Portsmouth, and Buford on Salisbury Plain.

Collection of 'Stars'

It was hard work for often we were out on the road by five o'clock in the morning – stern training for the rugby union football we had at the weekend. But it kept us fit and the Saturday matches really were most enjoyable. In addition to Clark, Gronow and myself, there were in this A.S.C. (Grove Park) rugby union team such Northern Union players as Jack Corsi, who then was with Rochdale Hornets, E. Ware, of Dewsbury, Frank Holbrook, of Oldham, Ernie Jones of Rochdale Hornets – he went on one Australian tour with me – Louis Corsi, also of Rochdale Hornets, his brother Joe, and Herman Hilton of Oldham.

Maurice Neal, who played for England Rugby Union, was an officer at Grove Park; there was Lieut. Cockell who had played for Merchant Taylors, Bert Winter, a Bath and Somerset County man, Lieut. Nixon a wing three-quarter from the Harlequins; another officer named J.W. Alexander who had played with Cambridge University, and later there arrived at Grove Park more Northern Union reinforcements in Albert Rosenfeld, Trevarthen, who had come over to England with the 1907 New Zealanders, and Dai John, the Salford full-back.

The Grove Park Army Service Corps (ASC) rugby union team: Back: Mellor, Jones, Holbrook, L. Corsi, Clark; middle: J. Corsi, Gabrielle, Alexander, Gronow, Pavine, Brown; front: Ware, Cockell, Neal, General Burn, Major Stanley, H. Wagstaff, Nixon.

A rare action photo of Harold Wagstaff, playing for the ASC rugby union team during World War 1. It was published in *The Tatler* on 28 March 1917.
(Both courtesy Robert Gate)

The team which had as its best formation: John, Rosenfeld, Ware, Wagstaff, Nixon, Cockell, Ernie Jones, Louis Corsi, Gronow, Hilton, Clark, Alexander, Trevarthen, Winter and Mellor, who played with Huddersfield Old Boys before the war, developed a wonderful combination – a team which played rugby league football under rugby union rules.

The rugby union men in the side learned that it paid to cut out kicking, to rely on passing and the result was that all sorts of movements were developed. We used to average something like 40 points a match and in other Army and Navy centres where rugby union teams had been set up, they did everything they could to get together a side to lower our colours.

13 Tries in a Match

We went to play a match with the Royal Engineers at Chatham, and any amount of betting on the result of the game was done by the officers. Anyway, Captain Nixon, who was on my wing, came to me before the match and said: "Wagstaff, we have to win this match and I have to score a couple of tries, otherwise three months' pay goes wallop."

I said: "Very good, Sir."

I knew that Nixon, who though somewhat on the light side was a very aggressive little footballer, could run. Nixon had not a lot of idea when it came to beating a man, but he would run as hard as he could, and I have seen him go with his 10 stones 10 pounds into a big full-back, and then jump up and dart over the line before the other fellow could get up.

The Royal Engineers had a fair number of rugby union men who had learned their football at Public Schools, and they were a well-built and well-equipped side. When we turned up, I told Ernie Jones that the 'Captain' wanted to score a few tries, and asked him to play to my wing as much as he could.

For about 10 minutes or so, the Royal Engineers gave us a hard game, and then we started. Five minutes from time Captain Nixon returned from the line after scoring his 13th try, and he walked straight up to me.

"Wagstaff," he said, "do I look like a fool?"

"No, sir," I replied

"Well, I must be one," said Captain Nixon, "because I am the only man in this side who is doing any running."

What happened, of course, was that the Royal Engineers kicked out after a try had been scored. A scrummage followed. Our forwards saw to it that we had the ball, Ernie Jones sent it on to me and I let Nixon have it, usually about the halfway line. Away he tore to score; and then the whole business was repeated again and again. Nixon scored over 80 tries that season.

We beat the Manchester Regiment at Colchester, in which there were a few Northern Union men, including Vivian Farnsworth; we had some memorable games with the New Zealanders, and we went on beating sides from the Army, the Navy and the Air Force.

Our colours lowered

When we played the Naval sides, we met such men as Harold Buck, Joe Brittain, Willie Davies, and Jack Beames of Halifax and then Captain Russell Cargill, who had said he would do the trick, picked the side which in the last five minutes of a grand game got the points to beat us 6–3.

The side chosen by Captain Russell Cargill was a team of all countries. There were Northern Union, Irish, Scottish, Welsh, New Zealand and South African internationals in it and in the pack was WW Wakefield, who was to make such mark in English rugby union football after the war. But we had a satisfying revenge, for some time afterwards we played the same team again – this time the match took place at Blackheath – and we won by 16–3.

Our Grove Park ASC team scored well over 1,000 points that season, and Ben Gronow, who with Douglas Clark, Louis Corsi and Herman Hilton, was so useful in the 'lines', kicked lots of goals. I believe he landed something like 200, and I know there was one match he missed in which Frank Holbrook, his deputy, kicked 20 goals. Mention of the way in which our Northern Union forwards learned to make play from the 'lines' reminds me of the first game in which I saw Douglas Clark ordered off the field. We were playing Oxford University cadets at Grove Park, and in their pack they had a bustling sort of a forward who weighed no more than 11½ stones, but who really was a nuisance.

Referee in error

One of those fellows who always had his hands swinging about, in the 'lines' he was an aggravating sort of a fellow, and he was just as troublesome in the loose. He caught me a blow in the face and though I knew he did not intend it, I was a bit worried as to what should be done about him.

Eventually I said to Douglas "I am surprised at you letting that little lad have things all his own way – look at the way in which he's throwing his hands about. Isn't it about time you reminded him that he is playing with men?"

Now, this player had a set of biggish pearl buttons at the neck of his jersey, and when Douglas took hold of the jersey collar, and with a Cumberland cross-buttock threw the lad seven or eight yards, the pearl buttons flew all over the place. The collar of the jersey stayed in Douglas's hand. Straightaway the referee ordered Douglas off the field. We were amazed, for there was nothing wrong in what Douglas had done.

At half-time, Douglas was still on the touch line with Major Stanley – he was ever so upset at being sent off – and we got the Major to ask the referee the reason for the drastic action taken. The referee's reply was that Clark had struck the Oxford man and knocked out a number of teeth.

The Oxford man turned up smiling to say that he was all right, and that he still had all his teeth. Then came the explanation. The referee had seen the Oxford man flying through the air, and he had seen the pearl buttons flying through the air as well, and he had jumped to the conclusion that Clark struck and knocked his teeth out. A comic business altogether, but poor consolation for poor Douglas, who had been sent off so unjustly.

A wrestling match

I could tell, if I had space, of a famous wrestling match at Grove Park, when Douglas, who was corporal in charge of the room in which Ernie Ware, Ben Gronow and I had places, tackled Ernie Ware and myself.

Ben refereed and the match took place on the wooden floor of an Army billet. It took us five minutes to get him down the first time, and over five minutes to get him down the second time and, though we won the match, Douglas had the laugh, for next morning at five o'clock, when it was time to get up, Douglas was just about as fit as could be while neither Ware nor myself could move. And in those days Douglas was not really interested in wrestling!

At the end of 1916–17, this Grove Park ASC team was broken up. I went to Egypt, Ernie Ware to German East Africa, Rosenfeld to 'Mespot', Herman Hilton, Jones, Clark, Gronow and the rest to different companies in France and there we stayed until the Armistice when, in next to no time, we were all gathered under Major Stanley's care once again.

Then all the talk had to do with the huge inter-Services competition that was to take place – the Rugby Union Championship of the forces for which the Army, the Navy, the Air Force, the Australians, the New Zealanders and the South Africans were preparing. It was plain, of course, that they could not keep many of us who had played Northern Union football before the war out of the Army side but before the competition was started, we were demobilized and so it happened that, instead of taking part in that rugby union championship, we Huddersfield men returned to Fartown to take part, as I have told in an earlier article, in Huddersfield's successful battle for the Yorkshire Cup.

Happy memories

Those rugby union days were happy days. I made many friendships which have survived the years that have gone since the war. Occasionally, letters reach me from Maurice Neal and one or two other rugby union men with whom I played then to remind me of the time when rugby league and rugby union men played together to the enjoyment of everyone. And now that the end of the season is near, I reach the end of my reminiscences. Next week I propose to conclude with the story of the 'Rorke's Drift Match' at Sydney in 1914 – the greatest test match I played in. But before I finish this week, I must tell of the shock we had when we got to Australia in 1914. Six of us had travelled on a later boat and we did not arrive until the Thursday before the Saturday on which the first match was played. Then we were beaten 36–10 by the Metropolis team, before a wonderful crowd of 60,000.

I saw Harold Horder play that day and I have never forgotten my first sight of him. I thought I had never seen anything like him, and I still think so. His swerve fascinated me, and, when I think of it my memory jumps from 1914 to 1920, when we started our tour in Australia. Then I saw Horder again, realised that experience had made him into a greater player than ever, and when I went out to play against him for the first time on that tour, I had a long talk with Gwyn Thomas in an effort to make a plan which would check Horder.

Brilliant Horder

We arranged that when Horder had the ball, we should endeavour to keep him on the touch line, the scheme providing for Gwyn being there on my left. Gwyn would have the touch line covered, and our belief was that when Horder swerved, he would swerve right into my tackle.

When Horder first got the ball in that 1920 match on the Sydney ground, everything to start with worked according to plan. I got my position, and Gwyn took his, and when Horder saw that the wing was closed he began his swerve from Gwyn towards me. But, and I still marvel at it, instead of swerving into me, or in front of me he swerved behind me.

I don't think I was ever so surprised in my life. I know that as he swept behind me in a swerve of incredible depth, I turned round helplessly to watch him go past and as I turned round my legs became crossed and twisted and I sank to the ground just as Horder shot under the posts. Gwyn Thomas had gone to ground in similar fashion and we looked at each other and said "Well, what you know about that?"

A great footballer, Horder, I often thought that the length of his legs and the shortness of his body counted for everything in his wonderful swerve. When you think of it, Horder in ordinary clothes looked about half the size he appeared to be in football 'togs'.

13. My greatest test match

"I have never seen the bulldog tenacity, the courage and heroic skill of the Englishmen that afternoon surpassed on the football field. That day Wagstaff, the English captain, played with inspiration that left upon my memory that it was the most wonderful game any man has ever played in the face of colossal odds.

Wagstaff, always a great player, that day became the ubiquitous, and the King of the game ... Here, there and everywhere, all the time he was doing the work of half-a-dozen men, inspiring his valiant band, dominated by misfortune, to transform themselves each into two men. Wagstaff the Great."

This is what JC Davis, the editor of *The Sydney Referee, wrote about the 'Rorke's Drift' match, the deciding test between England and Australia in 1914, played on the Sydney Cricket Ground.*

In the following article, the last in a series which has aroused interest wherever rugby league football is played, Harold Wagstaff tells his own story of the greatest test match in which he played.

The 1914 tour, the opening of which I told about last week, had a disastrous start. We lost the first two matches, and our football was poor because we were not fit. The newspapers were exceedingly rude about our work — talked about our football being like that of a lot of schoolgirls — and we had to be quick to do something about it.

I was called into conference by the managers, and my suggestion was that we should straightaway get down to it — that we should go to the ground every morning, have lunch sent there to us, and continue training in the afternoon until we had felt we had had enough.

Everyone in the side tackled the business keenly, and we made a quick and entirely satisfactory revival. It was a revival so satisfactory, at all events, that when the first test was played on the Agricultural Ground, Sydney, we were able to win comfortably.

Yet we took the field in that match without a regular full-back. Alf Wood had broken his nose and Gwyn Thomas had a fractured rib, and we had to play Bill Jarman, the Leeds forward, at full-back.

We went out that day determined to show the people of Sydney that we were not what they thought we were. A goal kicked by Longstaff from inside our half – the crowd jeered when he placed the ball, for they thought he had no chance – gave us a quick lead. We got 23 points and they did not get a point until the last five minutes.

23–5 was good enough.

Toll of injuries

The second test was played on the following Monday – it was the King's Holiday – and, because Jarman, Longstaff, Moorhouse and Bert Jenkins were injured, we were hard put to it to get a team.

Gwyn Thomas and Wood, the full-backs, were not fit. Francis, another of the backs, was out of the reckoning because of injury, and it was more or less a scratch side that we were compelled to field.

We were beaten 12–7, in a game in which we had our first experience of the substitution rule that was worked in Australia in those days, and so the position in the battle for the 'Ashes' stood one each. The arrangement was that the final test should be played at Melbourne when we returned from our trip to New Zealand.

An England versus New South Wales match had been fixed for Sydney the following Saturday, and on the Wednesday morning Mr J. Clifford, one of our managers, took a team up to Bathurst in the Blue Mountains. Then the Australians began an agitation for the third test to be played at Sydney in place of the England versus New South Wales game on the Saturday.

Mr Clifford was away and could not be consulted, and in the end, the Australian authorities cabled to England to ask the Northern Union Council to agree to the third test being played as the Australians desired.

The message from England

A special meeting of the Northern Union Council was called in England, they agreed to the Australians' demand, and they sent this cable to the English party in Australia: "Play match as Australians desire; England expects that every man will do his duty."

So, it came about that the third test was played on the Saturday following the first – just think of it, three tests in eight days for a tour team crippled with injury.

When Mr Clifford returned from the Blue Mountains to hear of what had happened, he was wild with indignation.

The 1914 British Lions: Back: J. Clampitt (Broughton Rangers), D. Clark (Huddersfield), F. Longstaff (Huddersfield), W. Roman (Rochdale Hornets), D. Holland (Oldham), J.W. Smales (Hunslet), W. Jarman (Leeds); standing: W. Hall (Oldham), G. Thomas (Wigan), J. Chilcott (Huddersfield), J.W. Guerin (Hunslet), A.P. Coldrick (Wigan), A. Johnson (Widnes), R. Ramsdale (Wigan), F. Williams (Halifax); seated: J. Robinson Rochdale Hornets), J. O'Gara (Widnes), S. Moorhouse (Huddersfield), WJ. Clifford (manager), H. Wagstaff (Huddersfield – capt.), JH. Houghton (manager), W.A. Davies (Leeds), A.E. Wood (Oldham), B. Jenkins (Wigan); front: A.E. Francis (Hull), J. Rogers (Huddersfield), D. Murray (trainer), F. Smith (Hunslet), W.S. Prosser (Halifax). (Courtesy Robert Gate)

Harold Wagstaff (on right) with the 1914 Lions tourists at Tattersalls Club. (Courtesy *Rugby League Journal*)

Anyway, Alf Wood decided to take the full-back position, though his nose was far from right, and we turned out with this side: Wood, Frank Williams, Hall, Wagstaff, WA Davies, Smith, Prosser, Holland, Coldrick, Ramsdale, Johnson, Clark, Chilcott.

The Australian side was: Hallett, Frawley, Deane, Tidyman, W. Messenger, Halloway, Fraser, Pearce, Sullivan, Cann, Craig, Courtney, Burge.

My first memory of the day on which that match, which came to be known as the 'Rorke's Drift' match, was played – if you look in the records in the Rugby League handbook you will see that while the other test matches are numbered, this one is distinguished by having (R.D.) alongside it – has to do with the fighting speech that was made to us by Mr J Clifford, who was so upset about the way in which the arrangements for the match had been rushed through behind his back.

Words of fire

He called the men who were playing that afternoon – the 13 of us – into a room in the hotel, and he outlined the whole story of the revision of the fixture. Then he said that he expected every one of us to play as we had never played before.

"You are playing in a game of football this afternoon," he said, "but more than that, you are playing for England, and more even than that, you are playing for Right versus Wrong. You will win BECAUSE YOU HAVE TO WIN. Don't forget that message from home: England expects every one of you to do his duty."

The men in my team were moved. I was impressed and thrilled as never before or since by a speech. You could see our fellows clenching their fists as Mr Clifford spoke, and I know that when we left the room, none of us spoke.

We were prepared to go all out when we went onto that field at Sydney; but before there had been a scrummage in the match Frank Williams, on the wing, had twisted his leg. We took 'Chick' Johnson out of the pack to help Williams on that wing.

We managed to lead at half-time by 9–3. Percy Coldrick had scored a try and Alf Wood had kicked three goals.

Immediately we started the second half, Douglas Clark smashed his collarbone. He had broken a thumb in the first half and it had been bandaged tightly so that he could carry on.

In the early stages of the second half, Clark got a pass and went racing clear of all, it seemed, for the line. But 'Pony' Halloway challenged him.

Douglas put out his hand to push Halloway off and then remembered the broken thumb. He withdrew his hand and went to

Halloway to give him his shoulder, but Halloway 'stalled' and Clark, unable to recover his balance fell on his shoulder and the collarbone went.

Douglas Clark in tears

He had it strapped and twice he made an effort to return to the game; but in the end he had to decide that it was impossible for him to carry on. There were tears in his eyes when he left the field for the last time.

Frank Williams hurt his leg again, and he had to go off and there we were left with 11 men. Then Billy Hall of Oldham, was carried off with concussion – he received his injury when he went down for the ball – and we had 10 men to face 13. Ten men and 30 minutes to go.

But never had I such nine men with me on a football field as I had that day. We were in our own half all of the time, and for most of the time we seemed to be on our line; but we stuck at it. Our forwards gave their all.

In the scrummages, the remnant of the pack that was left did its job, and, in the loose, the men who had been brought out tackled as fiercely and as finely as the backs did. 'Chick' Johnson was on one wing. Percy Coldrick was on the other wing and Willie Davies was in the centre with me.

As often happens in such circumstances, we continued to get the ball from the scrummages. Holland, Ramsdale and Chilcott were heroes.

There were 20 minutes left when I managed to make a cut through after taking the ball from Fred Smith and Prosser. I went to the wing on which was Johnson, and when I gave 'Chick' the ball there was only the full-back in front of him.

'Chick' went away with it; but then none of us dreamt that we were to witness the scoring of as wonderful a try as test football will ever produce. A few yards from Hallett, the Australian full-back, 'Chick' put the ball on the ground and began a dribble.

He had half the length of the field to go; but he went every inch of the distance. And the ball never left his toes. It might have been tied to his feet – a ball on the end of a piece of string – so perfectly did he control it.

Played to a standstill

No international Association player could have dribbled a ball better than Johnson did that afternoon on the Sydney Cricket Ground. Man after man he beat, until finally he tapped the ball over the line, and dived for the touch.

Left: A poster advertising newspaper coverage of the tour.
(Courtesy Robert Gate)

Alf Wood kicked the goal, and there we were 14–3. Billy Hall recovered and came back for the last 10 minutes to help us in a defence that was successful, until, in the last few minutes, Sid Deane scored the second Australian try.

But the victory was ours, and the Australian crowd gave us full credit for it. They swung round to our side in the second half, and they were with us to the end, cheering us on in inspiring fashion. When the final whistle sounded, we were done. We had gone to the last gasp, and were just about finished.

Some friends from Huddersfield had come to see us play, and when the victory was won, they produced some champagne, and never was champagne more welcome. I know that most of us stayed in our red and white jerseys and blue pants, content to sit resting thankfully for at least an hour after the match. We were simply too tired to make the move to the brake that was there to carry us back to our hotel.

We lost no more than three matches on that tour – the first two and the second test – and when we returned from New Zealand, we had to play New South Wales at Melbourne. Now this match at Melbourne was supposed to be an exhibition affair – a game to help the code in Melbourne, where there was little or no rugby league football.

But there were, I am afraid, old scores to be paid on both sides, and the result was that the Melbourne match was the roughest in which I have played.

An 'All In' match

I shall never forget the sight of the two packs standing up to each other in some real 'all in' stuff, with a tremendous crowd cheering like mad because they thought it was all in the game they were seeing for the first time. An exhibition game!

It was, however, the last of the bad matches. In those days, for some reason or other, we never seemed to get to know the fellows on the other side.

When you passed an Australian player in the street, neither of you thought about stopping for a chat. You just growled and walked on.

After the War, things improved enormously. The men on both sides mixed, became friends and learned to appreciate each other. Frank Burge, that great Australian forward, who played in the Melbourne match, always used to mention it when I saw him, and whenever he writes to me now he touches upon it, but he never fails to point out that, though we played in that match in which neither side squealed, we learned to become great friends, and great friends we still are.

I could go on for a long time writing about these Australian test matches, and about the international matches in which it has been my fortune and pleasure to play since I first represented England at Huddersfield on 1 January 1909. That season I played for England versus Wales at Coventry. I played first in test football in 1911–12, turning out at Newcastle and Edinburgh – that was the match in which Frank Renton over-ruled a touch judge regarding a goal.

I played first in test football in Australia in 1914, and I played in two of the three tests in Australia when I captained the 1920 tour team. Then, in 1921, I played in two of three tests when the Australian side, which included Duncan Thompson, Blinkhorn, Caples, Craig, Horder, Fraser, Burge, Pearce and the others, were over here.

I was in the side when at Salford in 1921 we regained the Ashes we have held ever since, and I can claim that I hold the Ashes.

After that match at Salford in 1921, the Australians made me a present of a silver cigarette case to commemorate England's victory in the Ashes, and when they gave it to me they placed in it, as a joke, of course, the ash from the cigarettes they were smoking.

I have many souvenirs of my football career. There are none I treasure more than that cigarette case and the football with which we played in the Rorke's Drift test at Sydney in 1914.

The 1920 British Lions: Back: D. Hurcombe (Wigan), E. Davies (Oldham), H. Hilton (Oldham), B. Gronow (Huddersfield), W. Cunliffe (Warrington), D. Clark (Huddersfield), F. Gallagher (Dewsbury), A.E. Wood (Oldham); standing: W. Reid (Widnes), G. Rees (Leeds), G.A. Skelhorne (Warrington), J. Cartwright (Leigh), A. Johnson (Widnes), J. Bowers (Rochdale H), E. W. Jones (Rochdale H), A. Milnes (Halifax); sitting: C. Stacey (Halifax), G. Thomas (Huddersfield), S. Foster (manager), H. Wagstaff (Huddersfield – capt.), J. Wilson (manager), J. Bacon (Leeds), S. Stockwell (Leeds); front: J. Parkin (Wakefield T), J. Rogers (Huddersfield), D. Murray (trainer), J. Doyle (Barrow), W.J. Stone (Hull) (Courtesy Robert Gate)

The leadership of the 1920 tour: John Wilson (tour manager), Harold Wagstaff (captain), Sydney Foster (tour manager), Gwyn Thomas (vice-captain). (Courtesy Robert Gate)

Huddersfield's tourists on the 1920 Lions tour: Ben Gronow, Harold Wagstaff, Johnny Rogers, Gwyn Thomas, Douglas Clark.
(Courtesy *Rugby League Journal*)

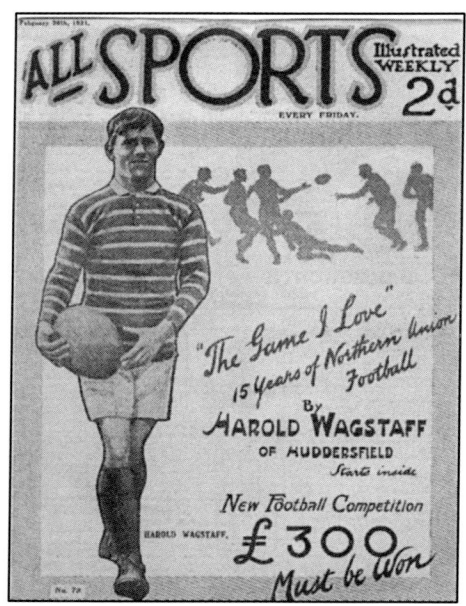

The cover of *All Sports Illustrated Weekly* promoting Wagstaff's series.
(Courtesy Robert Gate)

The Game I Love
Or 15 years of Northern Union Football

In the spring of 1921, Harold Wagstaff contributed a series of autobiographical articles to All Sports Illustrated Weekly. *There is a large overlap with the material from the* Yorkshire Sports *series included in this book. What follows are some excerpts of material not in the* Yorkshire Sports *series. Some of the language used in his reports of the tours would not be acceptable today, but it reflects the time that Wagstaff was writing in.*

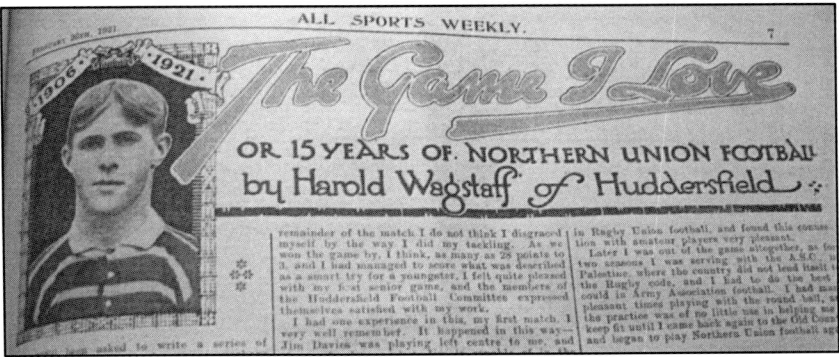

The heading of the series in *All Sports Illustrated Weekly* (Courtesy Peter Lush)

1906–07: About a Challenge Cup match with Warrington:

"Names to conjure with
At that time Warrington were a really great side, and in their ranks were men with names to conjure with. For instance, there was the great Jack Fish, the finest all-round wing threequarter the NU game has produced. Isherwood, his centre, was another brilliant player. Hockenhall, S. Lees, Taylor and some fine forwards, Boardman, Shugars, Thomas and others made up a great side.

I saw them beat Oldham in the Final for the Cup that season, when Jack Fish scored a most brilliant try after running practically the length of the ground, and all round the play of the Warrington team very greatly impressed me. We were to see more of Fish and his friends in later matches.

A Record Reverse
One match at Warrington, in which I did not play, was lost by Huddersfield by a total of 50 points or thereabouts, and this is the biggest total registered against the Huddersfield team since I have been

connected with it. In that match Jack Fish was in glorious form, and scored between 30 or 40 points himself." [Presumably this is the match on 20 October 1906, Warrington 50 Huddersfield 3. Fish scored four tries and nine goals for 30 points].

Wagstaff also writes about the players' pay in his first season:
"It may be interesting to recall how we were paid at that time. We backs got 25 shillings for a win, and 10 shillings for a loss or draw, and the forwards not being supposed to have the same value as the backs, had to be content with 20 shillings for a win, and 7 shillings and 6 pence for a loss. Fancy any first grade player being willing in either the Association or the Northern Union game to take such pay today!".

1908–09: Selection for the Yorkshire team

After the trial match: "Of the Huddersfield club, Percy Holroyd and myself were chosen to play against Cumberland in the first County match of the season. I was very jubilant at my selection for Yorkshire, but it seemed strange that Percy Holroyd, who was then 32 years of age, and had been a regular playing member of the Huddersfield club for a number of years, should only catch the selectors' eyes at this stage of his football career.

This was also Billy Batten's first County match, and he and I, except when out on account of injuries, have been in every Yorkshire County team since then."

1912–13: Support at Wigan in the Challenge Cup

"Having been drawn away in the first and second rounds of the Cup, we were hoping that the fortune of the draw would favour us in the third round, but you can picture our consternation when we found that we had to meet our most formidable rivals, Wigan, at Wigan. This match created wonderful enthusiasm in Lancashire and also in Huddersfield.

Many special trains were run, though it is a pity that a lot of enthusiasts from Huddersfield were unable to get into the ground, as the gates had to be closed half an hour before the kick-off. The attendance and receipts broke all previous records, there being well over 30,000 people present."

1913–14: Losing the NRL Championship Final

"The Huddersfield public were bitterly disappointed, and unpleasant rumours were flying round in all directions. It was said that the players selected for the [British Lions] tour were afraid of getting hurt, and so missing the trip, and that the other seven were so upset that they had not been given positions in the side, and that, between the two evils, we could not play for nuts."

The 1914 Tour

On becoming captain of the British Lions: "It was with much delight that I learned that Clark, Longstaff, Rogers and myself had been chosen for the tour ... the Northern Union asked me to captain the touring side [which] gave me great satisfaction.

I had only attained my majority at the time, and to have captained Huddersfield and Yorkshire, got every variety of medal possible in the NU game, and then, on top of all this, to be given the highest honour of all as captain of England, were achievements I could look back upon with the utmost gratification.

Within the space of six years, and at the early age of 21, I had realised all my football ambitions, and had created a record which would take some beating."

The trip to Australia by ship by the six players who did not travel with the main tour group: "We called at two of the Mediterranean ports. The first was Naples, where we had the opportunity of visiting the ancient ruins of Pompeii, which showed us a side of life that we could have no chance of seeing in our own country.

The second stop was Taranto, on the eastern side of Italy, and we now realised what a wonderful education travel is. Between these two ports we had passed in the dead of night the active volcano Stromboli, a lurid and glorious sight after the peace and quietness of our English homes.

Though it was so glorious in the Mediterranean, the call of the East had got hold of me, for I had always had a desire to visit eastern climes, and was eagerly looking forward to reaching Port Said where East meets West.

When learning geography at school, one generally gets a vision of what these places will be like. The coloured pictures of the natives in the schoolbooks may look very nice, but I can assure my readers that appearances are deceptive in this case, for my first visit to Port Said made me somewhat disgusted with the filthy conditions and dirtiness of the natives.

It seemed to me that during our brief eight hours stay in the town that every insect in the town had been mobilised, and they did not forget to make us aware of their presence, and we each felt as we boarded the ship that some of them had come to keep us company.

Some clever native conjurors came abroad here, and the way they fetched two chickens out of the boys' pockets left us all puzzled as to how it was done. The Egyptians are keen fellows at making a bargain. They would ask anything up to five pounds for an article which later you could buy for sixpence. Afterwards, during my Army life in Egypt and Palestine, I became more used to this method of buying and the queer ways of the Egyptians.

Before going through the Red Sea, we all bought new white duck-suits in preparation for the hotter climate. These were all ready-made clothing, and though the coats mostly fitted very well, the trousers took a great deal of altering before they looked respectable.

When we came to use these bottom-end garments we soon found out that Egyptian sewing was nothing like the good work of an English tailor and was not suitable for the vigorous exploits of six muscular athletes. However, with the aid of numerous kind ladies on board these suits sufficed to keep us in something like comfort for our journey through the tropics."

This account of the trip to Australia continued in the next edition: "When we left [Port Said] we had a 90 miles passage, which took 15 hours, through the Suez Canal, that great triumph of engineering science. It was a wonderful sight for some of our boys to see for the first time the desert which stretches on each side of the canal as far as the eye can reach, and which is very different from the green fields of dear old England.

Most of the voyage through the Canal was done during the night, and it was rather weird to see a black nothingness relieved only by an occasional palm tree. A few of the boys who were not at all familiar with the geography of that part expected to see wild animals in abundance.

It had been noticed that Alf Wood, one of our full-backs, had been peering into the darkness for a good while, and he was asked what he was looking for. He caused endless amusement when he replied that he was watching for the Lions to come down to drink.

I have been through the canal on three occasions, and I find it more pleasant and much cooler to go through by night, as the heat from the desert and the broiling sun make the air very close in the daytime.

In the morning we arrived at Port Suez, that pretty little place at the entrance to the Red Sea. Here again we were harassed by natives selling all manner of things, and ready to take advantage of us poor Englishmen.

The weather was now getting very hot, and when we reached the Red Sea it was very expensive keeping our lips moist. Our allowance on this trip was ten shillings a week on board ship – a very modest sum

– and this money was spent two or three times over by the most thirsty of the boys. However, it was only two or three days before we were out on the open sea again.

We had by this time got a sports committee together, and for the next few days we quite enjoyed ourselves. Tournaments for deck billiards and quoits, cricket matches and all kinds of gymkhana events such as apple-ducking, slinging the money, spar fighting and blindfold boxing, were organised, and the majority of the prizes were won by members of the team.

We also had some very fine concerts, which our boys greatly assisted by their hearty singing of popular chorus songs.

Our next port of call was Colombo, and we were all eager to stretch our legs after 10 days on board ship for though we had stopped at Port Said and Aden, no one had been allowed to land, and our exercise had been restricted to a much smaller space than was usual for NU footballers. So, at Colombo our chaps made the best of it. Though after walking about for a few hours they seemed tired, and were ready to avail themselves of the chief mode of conveyance in the place – the rickshaw.

To be dragged along by natives made our boys feel like lords of the manor, and we got a great deal of fun out of these rides. The races we had caused great excitement; each player tipped his driver a few shillings above the fare to get home first, and some betting on the result added to the interest.

Johnny Rogers, who was the lightest man of the party, had a big advantage, and won a pot of money rather easily. We were all pleased by our brief stay at Colombo, and would have liked it to have lasted much longer, but our journey was only half finished, and we had to continue on our way.

We had another 10 days to go before reaching the Land of the Golden Cross, and most of this time was spent in playing deck games and cricket matches during the day, and at night there were dances and concerts … We had great fun in crossing the line. We all had to pass through Father Neptune's Court, and be unceremoniously ducked in a huge tank of water. This our boys very much enjoyed, for a cold plunge was just what they had been wanting for a long time."

The trip home: "Our voyage home after the 1914 Australian tour was far from a happy one, as war had broken out, and we had to be constantly on the watch for the German raider *Emden* which was known to be in some part of the seas we had to pass through.

Travelling night after night without lights was very monotonous too, but at last we arrived in England, though the journey had taken a week longer than usual, to find not the peaceful country we had left, but the whole land in a state of upheaval.

Three of the touring side – Robinson, Roman and Jarman – were reservists, and had to report immediately on our arrival at Plymouth, and before many weeks had passed, the last two named had given their lives for their country."

Playing Association Football in Palestine

"The next two and a half years [after finishing his time in the ASC in London] I spent in Palestine, under General Allenby, helping to remove the troublesome Turks. Egypt and Palestine were not exactly suitable places to go in for rugby football, so during my spare time I turned out with the soccer team at centre half. At different times I was stationed in Jerusalem, Jaffa, Bethlehem, Gaza and the Jordan Valley. I enjoyed seeing the holy places and the sunshine, but did not like the insects who tormented us poor Tommies."

The 1920 tour of Australia

"I thought the touring side was a very strong one, but, be that as it may, we only managed to win one out of three test games. Like our cricketers, we also experienced 'barracking'. Good humoured banter is quite the rule, for while the English spectator takes his sport as seriously as the players, the Australian goes in for a lot of funny remarks at the expense of the players.

At first this is rather unnerving, as it is so different to home experiences. When a player misses a ball they shout 'Give him a bag'. If he is injured, they 'count him out', and fumbling passes causes the crowd to tell the culprit to 'go and play marbles'.

International games attract large crowds over there. A record crowd of 80,000 spectators was at the first test of the tour, and the gate receipts were over £6,000. Sydney Cricket Ground on that day was a sight to remember. I have been on a good many football grounds, association and rugby, in England, but I have never seen anything to equal this place, either from a player's or a spectator's point of view.

The referees' interpretations of the rules troubled us considerably, for it was very different from what we had been accustomed to at home. Indeed, in the second match of the tour, against New South Wales, we were quite at a loss as to what was the right thing to do, and three of our men were sent off the field for disputing the referee's decision. Needless to say, we lost the game, and by as much as 42 points to 6.

However, before the next match versus New South Wales, the managers and captains of the two teams and the referee talked over the matter, and came to a rather better understanding with regard to the interpretation of the rules.

We defeated New South Wales, but we lost the first test, which was played at Brisbane a week later, by 8 points to 4. This was not a brilliant game, but it was a very hard fought contest. The following Saturday the second test match was fixed to take place at Sydney and before a huge crowd of between 60,000 and 70,000 we went down as the result of a brilliant exhibition by the Australians, and we readily agreed that they thoroughly deserved their victory.

We were now anxious to justify our right to be considered an international side, and we trained very hard for the third test. We won this match by 23 points to 12. I was myself a looker-on at this game, the first big contest I had watched in Sydney, and in my opinion, it was a really good exhibition of NU football, and quite up to international standard.

However, the Australian barrackers thought otherwise, and criticised and made rude remarks to their own players. We quite expected a fair report in the press, but to our surprise the losers were told that 'they would have been beaten by a third grade team.'

We considered this was very one-eyed indeed, but at the banquet the following week, when we handed over the mythical 'ashes' to the President of the League, a lot of things were forgiven."

The 1921 Great Britain team that beat Australia 6–5 in the first test at Leeds:
Back: Albert Johnson (Widnes), Billy Cunliffe (Warrington), Joe Cartwright (Leigh), Edgar Morgan (Hull), Jack Price (Broughton R), Jack Beames (Halifax), George Skelhorne (Warrington), Sydney Foster (manager); seated: Billy Stone (Hull), Gwyn Thomas (Huddersfield), Harold Wagstaff (Huddersfield – capt.), Jim Bacon (Leeds), Squire Stockwell (Leeds); front: Johnny Rogers (Huddersfield), Jonty Parkin (Wakefield T).
(Courtesy Robert Gate).

The programme from Wagstaff's last test match.
(Courtesy *Rugby League Journal*)

Part 3: Reflections on Harold Wagstaff

Harold Wagstaff – The Prince of Centres
By Robert Gate

A Rugby Football Genius
By V.A.S. Beanland (December 1945)

A Union man – Wagstaff & the NU Players' Union
by Graham Williams

Obituary and Funeral Report
Huddersfield Daily Examiner

A Wagstaff Gate
Rugby League Review

Leadership
Rugby League Magazine and Rugby League Review

Harold Wagstaff
The Prince of Centres

"There were famous men in the Huddersfield and England teams in those days, but Waggy was the most famous of all." – George M Thomson, *The Yorkshire Observer*, July 1939

Like his great contemporary Billy Batten, Harold Wagstaff came from humble origins. He was born on 19 May 1891 at Underbank, Holmfirth, a small picturesque Pennine village a few miles from Huddersfield, which has now been immortalised as the setting for the long-running television comedy *Last of the Summer Wine*. His father Andrew had been born in Underbank but in the 1870s had moved to Rochdale to work as a mill hand and married a local girl, Hannah Rhodes, who was also a mill hand. Two of Harold's older siblings, Ann Eliza and Arthur, had been born in Rochdale, but the family's return to Underbank around 1881 meant that Harold and two other brothers, Young and Norman, were native Tykes. Andrew Wagstaff's occupation changed eventually from mill hand to painter's labourer so the Wagstaff household never enjoyed times of plenty. Harold's mother died in 1904 when he was not yet aged 13.

By that time Harold was rugby mad, having begun to play the game as a child with an old yeast bag stuffed with rags for a ball. He graduated to being a member of the Pump Hole Rangers, a team of youths who met at the village pump in Holmfirth and played against other groups of lads from the surrounding districts, often in farmers' fields without goals or pitch markings.

He was a big lad for his age but many of his playing colleagues and opponents were three or four years older. The game they played was Northern Union football, for the old rugby union game had been virtually wiped out in the area since the Great Schism of 1895. Even so, Harold Wagstaff later recalled that the feats of the 1905–06 New Zealand All Blacks had a profound effect upon him and his play-mates, even though none of them ever saw the All Blacks in action. The vibrant reports of their matches and the descriptions of their revolutionary tactics, which placed utter reliance on handling and team-work linked to an unprecedented athleticism in the work of the forwards, strongly influenced the young three-quarter's philosophy on how the game should be played. Another major influence on him was the open style of play employed by the Broughton Rangers team in the early years of the 20th century.

However, the young Wagstaff's primary ambition was to play for Underbank Rangers, who joined the Western Division of the Bradford

& District League in 1906, after previously being a member of the Huddersfield & District League. Such was the fever for football in those times that the Rangers would draw crowds of a thousand and more to their Bank End ground for the visits of teams such as Hebden Bridge, Salterhebble, Raistrick, Brighouse St. James, Marsden, Birkhouse Rangers, Slaithwaite Juniors, Thrum Hall and the reserve teams of Huddersfield and Halifax. By March 1906 Harold had achieved his aim and made his debut for Underbank a couple of months before his 15th birthday.

The start of the 1906–07 season saw the birth of an essentially new game. The Northern Unionists reduced teams from 15 to 13-a-side, the knock-on law was modified, direct kicking into touch was banned and the play-the-ball was transformed into a defining feature of the game.

Harold Wagstaff's first taste of the new rugby came on 8 September, 1906 and he found it delicious. Underbank beat Huddersfield St. Joseph's 26–5 at Bank End with Harold scoring the first try for Underbank under 13-a-side laws. He also kicked the first goal when he converted forward Arthur French's try and finished the match with three tries and two goals. The *Holmfirth Express* noted: "The new game is one of life and activity, and full of incident. Too many games in the past have ended with both sides nil. Under the new rules, tries and goals should be plentiful. Sheer strength will be at a discount, and speed with staying powers will count".

Although he was still only 15, Harold was attracting a great deal of attention. On 20 October he starred in Underbank's 10–2 victory at Birkhouse Rangers in the second round of the Halifax Charity Cup, scoring two tries and two goals. The referee George Dickenson, a former Halifax captain and Yorkshire forward, approached Harold after the game and asked him if he would like to join Halifax. Harold was keen enough but Halifax did not come back to him. Apparently, Dickenson told the Halifax committee of the youngster's talents the following morning, but on hearing that he had barely passed 15, they did not care to risk signing him, one of them famously but foolishly declaring, "We want men, not boys".

Huddersfield heard of Halifax's *faux pas* and Joe Clifford, of the football committee, displayed more sense, persuading Harold to sign for the Fartowners. The deal was done at Harold's uncle's pub, the *Druid's Hotel* in Underbank, and the signing-on fee was five gold sovereigns.

Having exchanged the red jersey of Underbank for the new-fangled claret and gold hoops of Huddersfield, Harold Wagstaff made his first class debut for the Fartowners at Bramley on 10 November, 1906. He was aged 15 years and 175 days. Only Bramley's Harold Edmondson, at 15 years and 81 days old, when he appeared against Bradford

Northern in 1919, has ever played at senior level at a younger age than Wagstaff. Coincidentally Edmondson and Wagstaff were to be team-mates at Fartown in the post-Great War period.

Harold Wagstaff retained vivid memories of his debut at the Barley Mow, particularly of his direct opponent in the centre. Harold at that time weighed almost eleven stones but opposite him was the famous veteran Albert Hambrecht, capped 18 times by Yorkshire between 1895 and 1901, under both rugby union and northern union auspices, a formidably hard-running player who topped 13 stones. Wagstaff recalled, "The first time that I went to tackle Hambrecht – I can feel the bump now when I think of it! If ever a youngster felt that he had been under a steam roller, I did. In junior football, if one looked hard enough at a man he would pass the ball. I tried the same trick with Hambrecht, and, when he made it clear that he was not going to be intimidated, I went in to tackle in, I am afraid, a somewhat half-hearted sort of way. One knee hit me under the chin, the other whizzed past my face. I went down with a foot on my chest, and I realised at once that the making of a tackle in senior football was a vastly different thing from the making of a tackle in junior football. Someone said, 'Get him sideways. Don't face him' Whenever I had to tackle again that afternoon I dived at Hambrecht's ankles."

Jim Davies, Wagstaff's co-centre, chided him for not holding one of his bullet passes and informed him that football was not a game for babies. However, the portents were good. Huddersfield won 28–11 and Harold scored a second half try, with a delightful cut through to the posts. The *Leeds & Yorkshire Mercury* reported that "he played finely and gave promise of becoming a capital centre".

The *Huddersfield Daily Examiner* was more verbose: "The other centre position was given to the new recruit from Underbank, who, I should say, is one of the youngest, if not the youngest player, who has ever represented the club. His handling of the ball was a long way from perfect, which, I imagine, was the result of nervousness, as he improved considerably as the game wore on. Apart from this, I was very favourably impressed by him. He was always in the right place, whether on the attack or defence, he is already distinctly speedy, kicks well, tackles well, and all the way through displayed a considerable knowledge of the game, and, when he gets over the weakness he showed on Saturday, will make a really first class player with luck, or I shall be much disappointed, for he has the build and physical attributes, and, what is more important still, he evidently possesses brain, and I fully expect him to go a long way."

Wagstaff did not appear in reserve team rugby until he was near retirement in 1925, but he was allowed to turn out in a few more games for Underbank. On 22 December, 1906 he played in the centre alongside his brother Young in a 10–3 loss to Halifax 'A' at Bank End in the semi-final of the Halifax Charity Cup and on Christmas Day he made his last appearance for his native club, playing brilliantly and "kicking some good goals" in Underbank's 47–0 rout of Marsden.

In 1906, Huddersfield was a club with high aspirations and a ground at Fartown prestigious enough to host county matches and major finals. They had been one of the aristocrats of rugby union in the north but since the formation of the Northern Union they had won precisely nothing. In Wagstaff's first season they finished 19th of 26 in the league table, which represented an improvement for in 1904–05 they had finished fifth in the old Second Division and only been saved from further degradation when the two division system had been abandoned for 1905–06, when they attained 11th place. The potential at Huddersfield was nonetheless enormous and crowd support would boom if a successful, attractive team could be assembled. By the time Harold Wagstaff became a Fartowner the seeds of success had been planted but it would take a few years for fruit to appear. When those fruits ripened Wagstaff was, as it were, the head gardener.

On his arrival at Fartown the club possessed some real talent – Jim Davies, a Welsh centre, who later became a great stand-off in the glory years, and Cumbrian winger-centre, Billy Kitchin, a future England cap, were the star men. There were others too, such as the veteran scrum-half Percy Holroyd and the elusive young full-back from Morecambe Jack Bartholomew, uncle of comedian Eric Morecambe, and a couple of rising forwards in Ike Cole, an international at 19, and Arthur Swinden. Many more, however, were needed to make Huddersfield a real force.

In the meantime, Harold Wagstaff continued to blossom. The training regime at Fartown quickly drove his weight up to 12 stones – he always maintained his best playing weight was 12 stones four pounds. The extra poundage to his 5 feet 11 inches frame, he averred, went onto his hips and thighs so he never looked as heavy as he was, retaining a slim waist. With that shape he maintained he was able to swerve and sway away from defenders more effectively than if he had been more heavily built.

Under skipper Fred Charlesworth, the 1907–08 saw Huddersfield rise four places in the league table to 15th. Harold's progress was faster than the team's. Crucially, his views on the game were reinforced by his encounter with the New Zealand All Golds at Fartown on 12 October, 1907. Albert Baskerville's tourists were breaking new ground as the first overseas visitors and their impact was immeasurable. Huddersfield lost 19–8 and Harold's eyes were opened wide as he watched and tried to counter the machinations of Lance Todd, who scored two stunning tries, Edgar Wrigley, George Smith and the wonderful Australian Dally Messenger, alias 'The Master'. The young centre was confirmed in his belief that the NU game produced too much kicking and not enough passing, that teamwork and support play were prerequisites for success and that forwards should be capable of joining in the open play.

The 1908–09 season was a turning point for both Huddersfield and Harold Wagstaff. The team shot up to fifth in the table under new captain Billy Kitchin, who topped the try-scoring with 32. A major signing was that of Edgar Wrigley, the New Zealand All Gold, who partnered Wagstaff in the centres, while the forward pack, still adept in dribbling, became renowned for its ability to handle. Its inability to win the scrimmages, however, was its Achilles heel.

Wagstaff's development had been so swift that he was chosen to play in a Yorkshire trial at Dewsbury on 6 October 1908. Remarkably, he decided that he would adopt a policy of not kicking at all during the trial, whatever the others did. It certainly worked. His team, the Possibles beat the Probables 20–13 and Wagstaff's performance "captivated the crowd". He was duly selected to play for Yorkshire against Cumberland on 17 October on his home ground at Fartown. Cumberland were despatched 30–0 and Wagstaff did sufficiently well to retain his position in the Roses match at Salford a fortnight later. A 13–0 defeat was the result, but experience against men like George Smith, the New Zealand All Black and All Gold, and the celebrated Welshman Bert Jenkins – an incongruous centre pairing for Lancashire – was invaluable.

Wagstaff's county debut caused a stir. Many of those who saw it could not believe that Wagstaff was as young as it was claimed. His physique and maturity of play belied his youth. So much controversy over the issue arose that a facsimile of his certificate of Baptism was reproduced in the *Northern Union News* on 14 November 1908. The fact was that he had made his county debut at the tender age of 17 years and 141 days, a record which still stands for Yorkshire. His county career ultimately encompassed 15 caps and did not end until 1923. The fact that there were no county games between 1913 and 1919 clearly robbed him of many more caps. His county cap was presented to him by Harry Lodge, a Huddersfield committee man and former club captain, on 5 December 1908 in the saloon of the railway carriage by which the Huddersfield team was conveyed to their match at Hunslet.

Within a month of that presentation Waggie was elevated to a higher plane. The first Australian touring team had journeyed to Britain and were to play England in an international at Fartown on 2 January 1909. Their tour had been disappointing in many ways but the team had not been defeated in representative fixtures, having beaten Yorkshire, Lancashire and the Northern Rugby League and three weeks earlier had drawn the first Ashes test match against the Northern Union.

Wagstaff and Huddersfield half-back Percy Holroyd were chosen to make their international debuts. Again, Wagstaff was setting records for at 17 years and 228 days old he became, and remains, the youngest English international of all time.

The game was a robust and bustling affair, which hung in the balance until the final minutes. The star of the match was Harold's centre partner, James Lomas, the English captain. Lomas was here, there and everywhere and played himself almost to a standstill – he was the benchmark for all aspiring centres in Edwardian England. Waggie had a good game too, showing many touches of brilliance. Australia led 9–8 at the interval, but a tremendous dribble by Wagstaff was capped when Percy Holroyd scored the try which gave England the lead. A further late try gave England a 14–9 victory.

The season continued to go well for Wagstaff, whose centre partnership with the aggressive, bull-like but clever Wrigley became a sore trial to other teams. The duo were the main cause of Huddersfield's 5–3 victory over the Australians on 20 February, 1909, the local paper reporting, "It is getting quite monotonous to say that Wagstaff and Wrigley were the pick of the home backs. They again stood out by themselves, and one or the other was responsible for the opening out of almost every movement in which the home backs took part, while they were both insatiable in their search for work and their grand defence it was that made the Australians' attack look weak on so many occasions".

A few weeks later Huddersfield were looking a good bet for a place in the Challenge Cup Final, but were held to a 10–10 draw by Wigan at Fartown in the third round, played before a ground record crowd of 28,053. The game was reckoned to be one of the best ever seen on the arena but Huddersfield were well beaten, 16–3, in the replay at a mud-bound Central Park.

The team was certainly developing on the right lines – two tourists, Albert Rosenfeld and Paddy Walsh, had been signed following the Kangaroos' game at Fartown and, during the 1909 close season, that forward of forwards Douglas Clark threw in his lot with Huddersfield. Other fine forwards in Bill Trevarthen, a 1907 All Gold, and Elijah Watts (Leeds) added to the club's burgeoning staff. These were men who could make a difference and Waggie was raring to go for the following season, when the first Lions tour of Australasia would surely be an attainable goal for the new international centre.

Sadly, his dream was shattered. Having played in the first three games of the season, all victories, Harold was taken gravely ill. He had grazed his knee in the opening fixture at Bramley and must have picked up some soil-born infection. The knee turned septic and general blood poisoning followed. He was taken to Leeds Infirmary and Huddersfield announced: "There is every hope of his ultimate recovery but his illness, we are afraid, will be a long and tedious one". So it was, and to make matters worse, he contracted mild diphtheria and was transferred to Seacroft Isolation Hospital. By January 1910 he was back in training, but suffered another leg injury and was not able to return to action until the end of March. Ironically Huddersfield had lifted their first major trophy, the Yorkshire Cup back in November and he had missed the historic event. By the time he returned to the playing ranks the Lions touring team had been selected and his hopes of touring had vanished. His club-mates Jim Davies and Jack Bartholomew had earned places, however.

It was not the end of the world. Wagstaff was still only 19 and he was to prove almost injury free in the coming years although he did periodically suffer severe illnesses. Huddersfield had reinforced their side even more. John Willie Higson, a member of Hunslet's 'Terrible Six' in their Four Cups side of 1907–08, the great Welsh second-rower Ben Gronow and Con Byrne, yet another All Gold, added massively to the forward strength. Tommy Grey, a superb Welsh scrum-half had been signed from Halifax and Wagstaff had a new partner on the left wing in Stanley Moorhouse. The two would terrorise opponents for many years to come. Even so, Huddersfield still flattered to deceive. They did reach the final of the Yorkshire Cup on 3 December and Waggy made his first appearance in a major final, but a dismal display ended in an 8–2 defeat by Wakefield Trinity at Headingley.

There was talk in the papers of a lack of 'esprit de corps' at Fartown and attendances fell, while some of the spectators who did turn up were proving unruly. The turn of the year, however, proved the making of the team. The last 15 league games ended in victories, several of massive proportions. Towards the close of the season the club made Harold Wagstaff, still not yet 20, captain, a position he was to hold, except for one season, until he retired in 1925. His own form through the season was tremendous. He won back his England place and confirmed his prodigious talent at Coventry on 10 December 1910, scoring a try and landing two conversions in a 39–10 drubbing of Wales. In the return at Ebbw Vale on April Fool's Day 1911, he partnered Billy Kitchin, who went over for two tries, while he scored a try and a goal himself in a 27–8 triumph. His display brought forth the following eulogy from the *Athletic News:* "Wagstaff by sheer skill and resource completely baffled such experienced defenders as Willie Thomas and Bert Jenkins. He was perfectly unorthodox and passed either inside or outside in a manner which made him the hero of the match … Never have I witnessed more perfect centre three-quarter back play, and the last try was a fitting termination to a game which will, I think, be regarded as Wagstaff's".

The 1911–12 season brought another Kangaroo touring team to Britain. Harold's test career began in a 19–10 loss against them in the first test at Newcastle on 8 November and he scored the only two tries of his test career in the second match at Edinburgh on 16 December in an 11–11 draw. Injury kept him out of the final test which resulted in a 33–8 defeat. The 1911–12 tourists were a much more successful team than their predecessors and Wagstaff was in losing teams on three other occasions against them, for England and twice for Northern Rugby League XIIIs. He had better luck with Huddersfield, however, helping his winger Stanley Moorhouse to a hat-trick in a 21–7 win at Fartown on 2 December 1911.

This was the point at which everything finally clicked at Fartown. Major Holland established himself at full-back and Fred Longstaff bolstered the pack. Wagstaff had the men to do the job and what a job they did under their inspiring leader. They won everything except the Challenge Cup, going down 2–0 at Oldham in the third round. The Yorkshire Cup, the Yorkshire League and the Championship were all lifted and only four league games out of 36 were lost.

Wagstaff had decided views about how he wanted his team to play. Huddersfield became known as the team which will not kick. Wagstaff had long been convinced that good passing was the most effective way of winning games. Kicking away possession, particularly on attack, was pointless. With good teamwork and constant support play, the ball could be taken forward without recourse to kicking for position. He had a collection of players of outstanding individual qualities but he knew that teamwork and team spirit were paramount virtues.

Somehow, he induced his band of extreme talent to subsume their individualistic tendencies for the good of the team. Result – brilliant football, big crowds, shoals of cups and championships, everlasting fame. Of course, the players had to be fit and trainer Arthur Bennett, who had been at Fartown since 1886, was a huge asset to the club. The importance of team spirit could not be overestimated. Wagstaff made sure no one missed team meetings, when "operational talks", as the players termed them, were delivered. He wanted a disciplined team but a happy one, in which all could depend on their colleagues. In his later career he was a leading light in the formation of a Players' Union. On the field Wagstaff was like a beacon to his team. Everyone on the ground knew that his force of personality dominated proceedings.

There was no doubt that he was a brilliant leader. He thought deeply about the game, could pinpoint teams' and individuals' strengths and weaknesses and was able to adapt tactics to any given situation. Albert Rosenfeld summed things up succinctly when he said, "All the players looked up to him. That's half the battle for a captain". Dinny Campbell, an Australian contemporary of Waggy and a superb centre for Leeds, believed he was the best captain the game had known, lauding him as "the greatest tactician I ever played against. His personality was dynamic". The journalist VAS Beanland was somewhat more poetic when he wrote in 1945, "He was the pivot of one of the finest scoring combinations I have ever seen ... He was never afraid of bustling methods when those methods were demanded, but it was his scheming brain that made him the great player that he was. He could fit in perfectly with any combination and was a master of the art of adapting his play to that of his colleagues ... If you watched him closely you would realise how perfectly he blended with his colleagues, how obviously he was the 'god in the machine', how deep was his knowledge of the weakness of the opposition, and how amazing was his intuition as to the right thing to do at the right moment".

To all intents and purposes Wagstaff had no weaknesses as a player. He had a robust physique, was a graceful runner with an exceptional swerve and could sidestep as well as most threequarters. His passing was wonderfully accurate and effective and he was a master at changing the direction of attack. He was totally unselfish, never gave his colleagues a ball unless they were better placed to progress than he. For a winger he was the ideal partner, his straight running giving the man outside him maximum opportunities and he would always take the bump rather than expose the winger to damage. He hardly ever dropped the ball, either in passing or in fielding kicks and his tackling was exemplary. Wagstaff often decried himself as one of the slowest men in Huddersfield's team, declaring some of the forwards were faster. His time over 100 yards was 11.5 seconds, but to onlookers he appeared quicker than he claimed. A career total of 209 tries indicate that he was no slouch. While he eschewed kicking, he was adept at it when necessary and his skill at dribbling was outstanding. Early in his career in a game against Leigh in very heavy conditions a ball was thrown to him from a scrum on his own '25'. It dropped at his feet and he dribbled it 75 yards, never attempting to pick it up, to score a sensational try. No Leigh player even touched the ball!

Always an innovative player, Wagstaff constantly sought different ways of breaking down defences. Towards the end of his first season as Huddersfield captain, he and Jim Davies devised a most famous manoeuvre – the standing pass.

The move produced innumerable tries, invariably on or towards the right wing. Wagstaff was a left centre and the move always followed a scrum. Grey would fire the ball to Davies at stand-off, who in turn passed to Wagstaff, who was already in motion when the ball arrived. He then ran dead straight to come up level with the scrum which had not yet broken up. This four yards dash was the vital element. Davies meanwhile had run to the outside of Waggy and was going full pelt.

Waggy would then pass orthodoxly to him or ship the ball over his shoulder to him, depending on where the opposing tackler was coming from. If it was the opposite centre he turned to meet the impact of the tackle with his right hip. If the tackle came in from the other side, he faced it and took the bump on his left hip. Opponents used to call the move scientific obstruction but, as Waggy asked, who was he obstructing? The only person suffering in the transaction was himself. He would later write, "It cost me a great deal of pain. I have come out of matches with my hips so sore that I could not put my hands on them, with hips so sore that the weight of my clothes seemed to hurt and sleep that night was almost an impossibility".

The 1912–13 and 1913–14 seasons produced almost unalloyed success to Wagstaff's Team of All the Talents. In 1912–13 only the Yorkshire Cup eluded them and in 1913–14 the Yorkshire Cup and League were both won, although defeat in the Championship Final by Salford was most unexpected. The team had added Johnny Rogers, the fastest scrum-half of his generation, and the fiery Australian centre Tommy Gleeson, to the back division, while Jack Chilcott and Aaron Lee had found places in the pack. Waggy himself had prospered. By 1914 he had become captain of England and when the second Lions team to Australasia was selected for that summer, he was the first man to receive an invitation. He was also awarded the captaincy. He celebrated his 23rd birthday just four days before the first tour fixture and remains the youngest man to lead a Lions tour to Australia and New Zealand.

The 1914 tour was the occasion of his supreme triumph. At extremely short notice and unilaterally the Australian authorities decided to stage all three Ashes tests within a week. The British tour managers protested, cabled home for instructions and were directed by the Northern Union, half the world away, to make the best of a bad job. The outcome was the most celebrated test in history.

On 27 June Britain routed Australia 23–5 at the Royal Agricultural Ground in Sydney. Two days later at the Sydney Cricket Ground an Australian 12–7 win levelled matters. The deciding test, on 4 July, also took place at the SCG. Britain had six players on the injured list and cock-a-hoop Australia fielded the team which won the second test. Within minutes Lions winger Frank Williams twisted a knee and later had to retire. Douglas Clark broke his thumb, but carried on until a dislocated collar-bone forced him off. In the second half centre Billy Hall was taken off concussed. Despite being reduced to 10 men, Harold Wagstaff marshalled his depleted forces so adroitly that they established a 14–0 advantage. The Australians managed to pull back to 14–6, but the gallant British held on to win the test and the Ashes. The game was dubbed "The Rorke's Drift Test" after the heroic action of a small British force against an overwhelming Zulu army in 1879.

JC Davis wrote in *The Sydney Referee:* "I have never seen the bulldog tenacity, the courage and heroic skill of the Englishmen that afternoon surpassed on the football field. That day, Wagstaff, the English captain, played with inspiration that left upon my memory that it was the most wonderful game any man has ever played in the face of colossal odds. Wagstaff, always a great player, that day became *the ubiquitous*, and the King of the game … Here, there and everywhere, all the time he was doing the work of half-a-dozen men. Wagstaff the Great."

'Arawa', in *The Sydney Morning Telegraph*, eulogised: "They say Inkermann was a soldiers' battle. So was this. For individual desperation no great match seen in Australia, or, perhaps, anywhere else, has equalled it. And standing out clear of all as the hero of his side and the day was the English captain, Wagstaff. Fine-looking, with an athlete's model frame, he was in everything, was everywhere, until at last he had the same effect on the Australian imagination as did Richmond on the distorted mind of Richard III. What a captain! He haunted the Australians. It was not Harold Wagstaff, the footballer, but Wagstaff, the Englishman, with his mind on a pole star. Never before has he played like this. One moment he was actually seen crashing into the scrum, to give his tired, hard-pressed vanguard a helping hand. Anon he was heading a desperate sortie on the left. A moment later he had come up in the centre, and then he was seen on the right supporting a forward who had broken away and fallen, dog-tired, by the way. Once, alone, he wormed, wriggled, twisted through half a dozen of them - a choice piece of work. And always he took the ball like an artist."

Wagstaff's men went through New Zealand unbeaten in six matches, but within days of the last fixture matters of greater import were on all minds. The Great War had commenced. It would claim the lives of three of the tourists – Walter Roman, Billy Jarman and Waggy's club-mate Fred Longstaff.

The Northern Union carried on as normal in 1914–15, apart from abandoning representative fixtures. Waggy and Huddersfield also carried on as normal. For the fourth consecutive campaign Huddersfield topped the table, losing only twice in the league. They swept all before them, at last emulating Hunslet's feat of taking All Four Cups in a season. They did it in far more style, however. Some have argued that it was easier for Huddersfield as the war took away many men at other clubs while the Fartowners only lost Jim Davies, who joined up straightaway. Whatever the case, Huddersfield were untouchable. After losing at Barrow in the league on 10 October, they were undefeated in the succeeding 39 matches. Even in the three finals, they simply annihilated their opposition – Hull by 31–0 in the Yorkshire Cup, Wigan 27–2 in the Championship and St. Helens 37–3 in the Challenge Cup.

After the latter game at Oldham, the *Yorkshire Observer* stated: "No club, in any age or any clime, has ever placed a team in the field which is comparable to the present Huddersfield combination, which has brought such lustre to the game".

The following season, however, the Northern Union abandoned competitive rugby. Wagstaff was a motor driver in civilian life and had married Ann Battye, a local Holmfirth girl, in January 1915, but now his world changed completely. In 1916 he was drafted into the Army Service Corps (ASC), seeing service in Egypt and Palestine (1917–18), where he played some soccer as a full-back. The ASC, which played out of Grove Park, was a top rugby union playing unit from 1915 to 1917 and Waggy became its shining light as it became the most successful team in Britain. It could hardly have been otherwise, containing as it did Huddersfield's Albert Rosenfeld, Douglas Clark, Ben Gronow and Bill Trevarthen, as well as several other Northern Union stars.

When peace returned Huddersfield remained the team to beat. In 1919–20 they topped the league and came within five minutes of lifting All Four Cups again. The Yorkshire League, the Yorkshire Cup and the Challenge Cup were all safely tucked away and the Championship Final against Hull was to take place at Leeds on 24 April. By that time, however, Wagstaff and four of his team-mates were en route for Australia. Huddersfield led Hull 2–0 only for a 75th minute try from Billy Batten to wrest the final accolade from them.

Wagstaff had again been selected as captain of the Lions. Although New Zealand were defeated 3–0, Britain lost the first two Ashes tests and Harold missed the 23–13 victory in the final test. By his own standards, his tour had not been quite up to scratch. Even so, he continued to play representative rugby until 1923. One of his greatest satisfactions was his leadership of the team which won back the Ashes in the home series of 1921–22.

His final test match was the decider against those Kangaroos at Salford on 14 January 1922. The conditions were appalling, snow and straw being the main ingredients of the pitch. Waggy never played in, and most of the onlookers never saw, a more strenuous match.

Britain won 6–0 and Wagstaff was carried in triumph from the field by a mass of invading fans but not before his mud-covered white jersey had been ripped to pieces by idolators seeking a relic of the great man's last test.

In 1923 Harold underwent an operation for a duodenal ulcer – he had suffered from stomach problems for several years – and afterwards played in a corset to protect his abdomen. He played on until 1925, making his last appearance in a first class fixture in the unaccustomed role of full-back in a 16–0 defeat at Oldham on Monday 23 March.

Huddersfield RLFC 1921–22: Yorkshire League winners. Back: A. Clayton (trainer), H. Lodge, T. Fenwick, W. Watts, F. Stamper, A.B. Canby, A. Swinden, J. Leeming, D. Clark, B. Gronow, A. Sherwood, J. Clifford, S. Abbey, S. Moorhouse, H. Bennett (assistant trainer); front: J. Rogers, A. Davidge, S. Williams, G. Thomas (captain) J. May, D. Jessop, H. Wagstaff, J. McTighe. (Courtesy Robert Gate)

A couple of months earlier he had become licensee of the *Boar's Head* in Halifax. In 1925–26, he became coach at Halifax but his tenure was short and unsuccessful and he joined the committee instead, serving on the football and finance committees. In 1931 he returned to Huddersfield to take over the *Royal Swan Hotel*. He dallied again with coaching when he took over the reins at Broughton Rangers in 1935–36 but it was a short-lived dalliance. His last association with the game was as a committee-man at his beloved Fartown.

Harold Wagstaff died on 19 July 1939, aged only 48. On the day of the funeral Westgate, in the centre of Huddersfield and the street on which Wagstaff's hotel stood, was lined by hundreds of people, who made the thoroughfare almost impassable for fully half an hour, a squad of police officers having to direct traffic.

At the funeral service at Holmfirth Parish Church, the vicar, the Rev. TH Cashmore echoed the feelings of the congregation when he said, "Holmfirth was rightly proud of a man who, in his own sphere, had carried her name far beyond their hills and valleys. He had great qualities of heart and mind and body that won for him the confidence and admiration of thousands."

Eight of Waggy's old playing comrades bore the coffin – Douglas Clark, Wimpenny Brook, Hartley Hirst, Stanley Williams, Ben Gronow, Billy Kitchin, George Todd and Major Holland. On the coffin lay two wreaths – a cross from his widow and son, and a model of a rugby ball made of golden lilies and claret carnations, which bore the inscription: "From the boys of the Fartown football team".

Jim Tranter (Warrington – on left) and Harold Wagstaff in 1921.
(Courtesy Robert Gate)

Harold Wagstaff and Halifax's Stuart Prosser shake hands, probably during the 1922–23 season. They were team-mates on the 1914 Lions tour.
(Courtesy Robert Gate)

A Rugby Football Genius

The temptation to become lyrical when the name of Harold Wagstaff is mentioned in connection with rugby football has to be resisted.

As an interpreter of centre threequarter back play Wagstaff was a genius, and it was rugby union's loss that he belonged entirely to the opposition camp, except for those years of the first great war when he was so distinguished a member of the Army Services Corps team that overwhelmed all opponents in the South ... London and the South had the opportunity that season of examining the claim of the North that Wagstaff was a quite outstanding centre in his day and generation, and the knowledgeable critics endorsed that claim with sincerity and enthusiasm.

Many rugby men of long experience regard Wagstaff as the greatest centre threequarter of all time. That is a tremendous claim when one thinks of grand players of the home countries, of Ireland and South Africa, of New Zealand and Australia one has seen under two codes of rugby in the last half century. Yet as I saw him in the season of 1913–14, when he and his fellow threequarters of the Huddersfield club scored 197 tries, I would pick him as one of my two centres in a world team, even remembering HH Messenger of Baskerville's New Zealanders who played in the Northern Union area here in 1907–08, WJ Wallace of the first All Blacks, Gwyn Nicholls of Wales, GV Stephenson of Ireland, those great old-timers of the three threequarter days, Rawson Robertshaw and FHR Alderson, and R Wilson and James Lomas of the Northern Union and Rugby League, a select little company that is representative of the most finished centre threequarter play of my time. ...

But sometimes more than a bald recital of achievement is necessary to assess the value to rugby football of Harold Wagstaff as I knew him in his playing days and long afterwards when he addressed himself to the task of writing instructive articles and toured the rugby union grounds of Lancashire and Yorkshire as a valuable commentator and critic of a game he held, as I know from many chats with him, in great affection. In those later years Wagstaff did very much in a quiet way for the rugby union game. He was always kindly in his criticisms; he was never assertive; and those of us who so often saw that big, quiet, unassuming man gravely watching the immature efforts of his successors on the field, found it hard to believe that not so many years ago his was the most keenly watched and admired figure on all the grounds on which he played ... I would attempt to picture Wagstaff as I knew him when he was, the pivot of one of the finest scoring combinations I have ever seen.

Huddersfield RLFC 1924–25: Back: J. Rogers, T. Fenwick, R. Cracknell, W. Watts, J. Hampshire, J.W. May, H. Wagstaff, F. Stamper, D. Clark, J. Brook, A. Sherwood, F. Merryweather (trainer); front: A. Walker, S. Williams, J. McTighe. (Courtesy Robert Gate)

The tall, slim lad of earlier years had developed into a man of fine physique, but it was as a tactician rather than as a robust thruster that he earned his laurels. He was never afraid of bustling methods when those methods were demanded, but it was his scheming brain that made him the great player he was. He could fit in perfectly with any combination and was a master of the art of adapting his play to that of his colleagues. His wonderful understanding with his fellows of the Huddersfield team was a joy to see. For sheer artistry he reminded me very much of Wilson, of Broughton Rangers, in earlier years. Where the powerful James Lomas dominated a game – you could see no one else when Lomas was in form – Wagstaff fitted quietly and unostentatiously into his side, and if you watched him closely you would realise how perfectly he blended with his colleagues, how obviously he was the "god in the machine", how deep was his knowledge of the weaknesses of the opposition, and how amazing was his intuition as to the right thing to do at the right moment. ...

He was a whole-hearted believer in straight running down the middle to give his wing man room, and time and again one has seen him straighten the attack from the centre when the out-half back has failed to make a forward move and beat his man. His chief maxim was, however, I think, that useless kicking is a crime. What a coach he would have made for the England rugby union backs of late years! What a wonderful player he would have been for his country had the fates decreed that he should blossom in the rugby union camp!

Harold Wagstaff leading out Huddersfield.
(Courtesy Robert Gate)

The programme from Wagstaff's benefit match.
(Courtesy Robert Gate)

Left: Wagstaff after he had retired from playing.
(Courtesy Robert Gate)

Below: Wagstaff with an amateur works team.
(Courtesy *Rugby League Journal*)

Harold Wagstaff

will be glad to see old
and new friends at the

Boar's Head Hotel,
SOUTHGATE.

Where Footballers Meet.

SHIRE ALES & STANDARD STOUT

| Telephone | Headquarters: |
| No. 3613. | V.A.F. & M.H.A.R.A. |

Harold Wagstaff,

ROYAL SWAN
...HOTEL...

Westgate, Huddersfield.

Telephone 1793.

Most Up-to-date Hotel in Town.

FULLY LICENSED.

Adverts from Halifax (top) and Huddersfield match programmes promoting Wagstaff's new career as a landlord – 1930 (top) and 1935.
(Courtesy Robert Gate)

A Union man – Wagstaff and the NU Players' Union

Over the NU's first quarter-century there had been no shortage of issues when it seemed that the collective voice of the players could have been heard to good effect. Many players had realised the benefits that such a move could bring pre-war but none of the initiatives had come to fruition. In the aftermath of the greatest conflict in human history there was a new resolve to bring together the players as a force for the good of the game.

The attempts to build a trade union for the NU players should be seen in the context of the post-war radicalisation of the working class, both in Britain and internationally. Many NU players, particularly in the mining industry, would have been involved in their trade union at work and at times taken industrial action. That they developed this approach into the sport that they were paid to play is not surprising.

The new domestic season was well underway when the Australasian touring party steamed into European waters in mid-October 1920. Harold Wagstaff, the captain, was the most prominent of a group of those tourists who had decided to throw their considerable weight into doing something positive to advance the status of the game's players. Among the others were his Huddersfield team-mate and tour vice-captain, Gwyn Thomas, and Albert 'Chick' Johnson of Widnes, all three of them tourists twice over. Once home, they immediately set to work convincing their fellow professionals of the rightness of their plans.

Most of them met up again at the Grosvenor Hotel in Manchester on Wednesday 10 November. Harold Wagstaff took the chair as players gathered from every senior club. Those present formed the NU Players' Union and agreed its aims as

1) The promotion of a spirit of comradeship among the players
2) To redress grievances
3) To obtain a modification of the laws governing transfers
4) To obtain benefits for players after a fair and fixed term of service

The knowledgeable and experienced group of players who lay behind the new venture now had to prove that they had the political skills to lead a trade union. Harold Wagstaff was elected as chairman and Gwyn Thomas as secretary. A committee of four – 'Chick' Johnson (Widnes), Arthur Skelhorne (Warrington), George Rees (Leeds) and the only non-tourist Jim Lyman (Dewsbury) – completed the Union leadership. There was a joining fee of 5/- (£0.25) and there would be a weekly subscription to be set later by the committee.

After some alterations had been made to its rules the Players' Union was recognised by the NU early in the New Year. Recognition, however, was not unconditional. To calm the fears of those within the NU who opposed that decision it was made clear that while the Players' Union could register as a trade union, recognition would be withdrawn if the Union pursued its intention to join the General Federation of Trades Unions. This organisation was a federation of craft and industrial unions. It still exists today, and among its members are the Professional Footballers Association, the Professional Cricketers Association and the League Managers Association.

With recognition by the NU secured and with players joining the new Union in significant numbers, its leadership set about drawing up its first list of demands.

Wartime inflation had caused disputes over wages to break out across the country. They had spilled over into the NU but that militancy was confined to club level; match payments were the domain of individual clubs and they were left outside the Union's main campaign. Surprisingly, there was no attempt to renegotiate the NU contract regulations, introduced in 1912 and 1913, stipulating that player payments were to be made solely on a match basis, that summer wages must not be paid and that outside employment had primacy. It appears that those tailored changes were designed to ensure that the NU's clubs were not liable and its professionals were not covered by the 1906 Workman's Compensation Act. To challenge that, a test case would have had to be taken to court and it is doubtful whether the NU would have been willing to grant approval for the Union to take that course of action at the outset. It was a significant impediment to the day-to-day support for the injury compensation claims, insurance cover and wage disputes of an effective trade union. In the meantime, the Union would have to find other ways to make a difference to players' lives.

Relations seemed harmonious enough to begin with. A match between teams representing Yorkshire and Lancashire for the benefit of the Players' Union was approved by the NU and held at Halifax on Monday 19 September 1921. The match was treated as an unofficial trial ahead of the Ashes' series, but a number of withdrawals, including Harold Wagstaff, Jim Bacon, Squire Stockwell, Sid Jerram, Danny Hurcombe and Frank Gallagher reduced its value. The crowd of around 7,000 were able to enjoy a spectacular nine-try exhibition which Lancashire won 29-22.

The next day the Union got down to some serious negotiations in Manchester. These focused only on the NU's centrally set wage levels. With the Kangaroos already in the country time was of the essence in agreeing terms for the upcoming representative matches. A three-man deputation – Harold Wagstaff, Gwyn Thomas and Salford's Willie Thomas – presented the Union's claim for a £10 fee for all representative matches. After discussion, this was watered down to £7 for test matches, £5 for other internationals and £3 for Cumberland county matches which were the responsibility of the NU. It was recommended that the Lancashire and Yorkshire County Unions should also pay the same fee. They agreed and those leading players selected received the higher fees against the touring Kangaroos. The payments were made possible by the NU's decision to set the minimum admission charge for the tour at 2/- (£0.10), double that charged a decade earlier.

On 16 February, the NRL's member clubs held a meeting to consider the first claim submitted by the Players' Union the previous week. The Union's proposals restated its aims to reform the benefit and transfer procedures of the NU. Firstly, all players should have the right to a fixed benefit or a bonus in lieu which should be compulsory after six years of service. Secondly, the operation of the transfer rules should be amended so that a player had a right to request a transfer if he had not been selected through no fault of his own for eight weeks and receive a percentage of the fee depending on his length of service up to 100% after six years. All those points were considered and the consensus was that the more frequent benefits, possibly amounting to three per season, and a share of any transfer fees would to be far too expensive and were rejected unanimously by the clubs.

Progress was made on some inexpensive but important elements of the Union's proposals to modernise the transfer system. Club retained lists would be reduced from 100 to a maximum of 75 players. A player placed on the transfer list should have his fee fixed and not be auctioned. An open to transfer list should be circulated by each club at the season's end. A board of appeal should be established to consider player complaints that a transfer fee was set unrealistically high. That final point was accepted but the Union's request for a seat on that board was rejected by 23 votes to 2.

On Monday 6 March, the Players' Union held a conference in Manchester, Harold Wagstaff presiding. After the conference, which lasted over three hours, Gwyn Thomas informed the press that it had been decided to ask the NU Council to receive another deputation and to reconsider the NU's original proposals. However, the news emerged the following day that the conference had also reached a decision that after a certain period they would refuse to play with or against non-members. Interviewed by the *Yorkshire Post*, Harold Wagstaff stated it was the intention of the Union to bring all non-union members into line and that most of the first and second teams of first class clubs were already members. It was the case that in one of those clubs two players were not members and in the other a few players had allowed their memberships to lapse. In a separate interview John Wilson stated he was unaware of this decision which in his opinion was a direct challenge to the authority of the game's ruling body.

One of those clubs must have been Wakefield Trinity for its secretary received a letter from the Union on 9 March stating that their members would not play against the club until the players in question had paid up their arrears. This had to be done by 27 March. Trinity's committee replied stating that they would select on merit and that arrears or Union membership would not be a criterion. In response to the letter, the NU Council meeting on Saturday 12 March decided that non-payment was entirely a matter between players and their Union and unless the Union withdrew the threat not to play against non-members at once recognition would be withdrawn. By the following weekend the Union announced that those members in arrears had signified their intention to pay and that therefore the strike threat was withdrawn. At the next NU Council meeting, in Manchester on 27 March, it was decided that there were no grounds on which it was possible to reopen negotiations on the Union's proposals.

With negotiations apparently concluded the Union called a meeting of members in Manchester on 10 April. Needing to address press reports that a strike to protest the NU's intransigence had been discussed for the day of the NRL Championship semi-finals (22 April), Gwyn Thomas stated that "it was never proposed or thought of by the Players' Union. We repudiate the story entirely." He went on to state that the Players' Union intended to adopt a more conciliatory attitude towards the NU. As a step in that direction the demand for compulsory benefits had been dropped; they would remain at each club's discretion. It was also the Union's intention to make responsible claims in other directions, including the reformation of their proposals in a modified form.

Two weeks after the NU had renamed itself the Rugby Football League (RFL), John Counsell, the newly elected chairman, opened the first annual conference of that body at Keswick on 30 June. The post-war economic boom was waning, times were getting harder and Counsell painted a depressing picture of the economic situation. Commenting on the heavy losses sustained by many clubs including his own, he said "the time had arrived for a substantial reduction in playing terms, in view of such losses, the industrial depression and reduced earning capacity of followers of the games." It was a clear warning from a director of Wigan, a club that had recorded a loss after being profitable for the past two decades, to the Union's leadership.

At its AGM on Saturday 12 August 1922, Harold Wagstaff tendered his resignation as Union chairman due to the demands of his motor haulage business, which he ran in partnership with Ben Gronow. Wagstaff's influence was further reduced when, shortly afterwards, he caught diphtheria and had to be hospitalised. 'Chick' Johnson was elected as the new chairman. At a difficult time, the Union had to try and make progress without one of its two most influential leaders. There was little sign of that more conciliatory attitude once the meeting got underway. It was decided to send a letter to the RL Council stating that unless it re-opened negotiations on the proposals submitted the previous season it would call a strike beginning on 26 August to coincide with the opening of the new season. In an interview given to the *Yorkshire Post* and published on 23 August, Gwyn Thomas said this course of action had been forced on the Union because the Council had turned down numerous applications for a meeting.

In response, the Council let it be known that as far they were aware nothing had changed since their previous rejection of those proposals. Such a hard-line on the Union's part was not universally popular; the press reporting that members at some clubs were not willing to take strike action. While the threat of a strike remained, the Council would not agree to meet, but accepted a form of arbitration. With both committees in separate rooms, meetings took place between John Wilson, the RFL secretary, and 'Chick' Johnson, the Union chairman, at a hotel in Manchester on 24 August. Enough progress was made for the strike threat to be called off, clearing the way for the full RFL Council to take part in serious negotiations in Leeds on 27 September.

In the middle of this tense situation the Union found time to support a player benefit. An unofficial Lancashire XIII met a Players' Union XIII at The Cliff, Broughton Rangers' ground, on Wednesday 6 September to support the joint benefit of Tom Danson and Salford's Harry Launce. Harry Launce had recently retired as Salford's full-back while Tom Danson was the former captain of Broughton Rangers. Danson had suffered a shoulder injury in the 1921 Lancashire Cup final. The injury had proved so serious that Danson had been forced to give up playing and was unable to work for a long period. Unfortunately, the attendance was described as being a "mere handful" to see Lancashire record an easy win 26–13.

Two weeks before the meeting with the RL Council, Gwyn Thomas submitted the Union's proposals which now only included two substantive items for negotiation. Still seeking to amend the transfer system to provide some gains for both player and club, it proposed that a transferred player should receive a quarter of the fee irrespective of length of service and that a seat on the transfer board of appeal be allocated to the union. After the earlier acrimony, the Union delegation – Gwyn Thomas, 'Chick' Johnson, Harry Heaton (St Helens), Alf Tomkins (Oldham) and Percy Coldrick (Wigan) – were well received and a friendly discussion ensued. The meeting concluded with the RL Council's decision to call a special meeting with representatives of all 27 NRL clubs on 19 October.

On the day that most of the NRL's members gathered in Manchester came vindication for one small aspect of the Union's work to date. Over the previous season Dewsbury had run up a big loss. One of the ways to cut the deficit was for the club to place its most prominent player, Frank Gallagher, a 1920 tourist, on the transfer list. That was during the close season at the unprecedented fee for a forward of £1,000. There was no interest and Gallagher invoked the transfer fee appeals procedure. His argument that the fee was too high was accepted and it was reduced to £600. The new figure proved a more accurate market assessment and Gallagher would finally sign for Batley while the clubs prepared to deliberate. Many more disgruntled players would follow his lead over the years to come.

At the meeting, the poorer clubs attempted to block the Union's demands saying they could not afford both benefits and a share of the transfer fee. To make progress it was made clear that a share of the transfer fee would only apply in the case of a first transfer. After a long discussion the principle of a player receiving a share of the transfer fee was carried 12-10. However, this narrow margin indicated the proposal would almost certainly not receive the necessary two-thirds support at the next RFL AGM. At this critical time, Gwyn Thomas fell seriously ill and was forced to sit out nearly all of the next five months.

Negotiations had reached an impasse. New blood and fresh initiatives were needed to take the Union forward but neither seemed a possibility. Inevitably support for the Union among the members began to wane. Although still battling his way back to health and fitness after a surgery on a stomach ulcer, the Union's affairs were once again placed in the hands of Harold Wagstaff. With momentum and members ebbing away, it was decided to wind up the Union. Gwyn Thomas split up the remaining funds amongst the various clubs in proportion to the subscriptions paid in. When the winding up was complete in May 1923, Harold Wagstaff arranged for those sums to be distributed through the clubs.

Those heady plans first talked over as they made their way through Australasia three years earlier lay in tatters. It was a sad end to an endeavour that had failed to achieve nearly all of its loftier aims. To end in such a manner meant there would not be another attempt to launch a Rugby League trade union for over 20 years. Once again it proved to be a short-lived affair. In the absence of an effective players' organisation, progress on the Union's outstanding proposal, to reform the transfer system to the player's benefit, would not be forthcoming until 1958.

Harold Wagstaff Obituary

From the *Huddersfield Daily Examiner* 19 July 1939

Sportsmen in all parts of the north of England will learn with great regret of the death of Harold Wagstaff, the 'prince of centres' and the former England and Huddersfield rugby league captain, which occurred this morning at a Huddersfield nursing home at the age of 48.

Wagstaff had not been in the best of health since the end of last year. More recently he had a bad attack of influenza, and this had left him with heart trouble and in a weakened state. He went into a nursing home on Monday and gradually became worse as complications ensued, passing away this morning.

Wagstaff was born at Underbank on 19 May 1891, and his first game with Huddersfield was at Bramley on 10 November 1906, when he was 15 years of age. So much controversy was aroused at the time by the youth of the brilliant new player that once in the official programme issued by the Fartown Club there was a facsimile of Wagstaff's birth certificate.

Honours came in the way of this young centre very soon, for when only 17 years of age he played for the County against Cumberland at Fartown and in the Yorkshire v. Lancashire match at Salford. From that time until 1920–21 except when unfit he took an active part in all the numerable international and Yorkshire County matches. Wagstaff was captain of the side sent out by the Northern Union in 1913–14 to Australia, and he regarded as one of the greatest matches of his career England's magnificent victory by 14 points to 6 in the last test match of the tour, the victors being two men short practically all the second half. When another British side toured Australia and New Zealand in 1920–21 Wagstaff was again captain, and he had with him four other Huddersfield players – Ben Gronow, Johnny Rogers, Gwyn Thomas and Douglas Clark.

Great scoring record

Wagstaff became captain of Huddersfield in 1911, when they won the Championship and again in the following season when they won both the Championship and the Northern Union Cup. In 1914–15, when the Fartowners again carried off both the League and the Cup trophies. Wagstaff, who had again been selected as captain, played a big part in the high scoring record set up by Huddersfield, who compiled 888 points in league games – an aggregate of 1,224 with cup and other games. The threequarters had 197 tries distributed among them as follows: Rosenfeld 55, Moorhouse 48, Wagstaff 34, Todd 33 and

Gleeson 27. The half-backs, Rogers and Ganley, scored 26 and 17 tries respectively.

During the War Wagstaff was one of the famous band of Army Service Corps footballers got together by Major Stanley at Grove Park. When the War was over Wagstaff returned to Fartown, and in 1920 Huddersfield once more gathered the RL Cup, beating Wigan in the Final at Headingley 21 points to 10.

Club achievements

His full record (club only) for the various seasons he had been associated with Huddersfield is:
14 goals, 185 tries, 583 points. [see Appendix]

£1,000 benefit

On 31 January 1920, Wagstaff took a well-deserved benefit in the Huddersfield versus Rochdale Hornets match at Fartown, when the chairman of the Huddersfield club (Mr Harry Lodge) wrote: "Always faithful to his club, ready to do a good turn for the game, for a club or for a fellow player, Harold Wagstaff has the best wishes of all supporters of football who sincerely admire a great player, one who has been a credit to his game and his club on and off the field." His popularity was such that a thousand pounds was taken at his benefit match.

Chaired from the field

Wagstaff, who was rightly proud of the distinction that he had never been sent off the field for unsportsmanlike behaviour, has been the subject of many remarkable demonstrations, not the least interesting of which was one that happened at St Helens. The home team were beaten by Huddersfield and Wagstaff was so much the outstanding figure of the match that at the end the St Helens supporters cheered him wildly and carried him off the field shoulder high. He was the subject of a similar demonstration when the English side of which he was captain, defeated Australia in the last test match in which he took part.

Wagstaff's test match appearances are as follows: Newcastle 1911, Edinburgh 1912, Sydney (1) 1914, Sydney (2) 1914, Sydney (RD) 1914, Brisbane 1920, Sydney (1) 1920, Leeds 1921 and Salford 1921.

He retired from the game at the end of the 1924–25 season, his last match with Huddersfield being on 14 April 1925. He retired to take over the licence of the Boar's Head, Halifax – though this did not by any means end his association with football. The Halifax club for a season or so engaged him as a coach, and later Broughton Rangers club after their re-organisation and their move to Belle Vue in 1935, engaged him in a similar capacity.

He returned to Huddersfield a few years ago to take over the licence of the Royal Swan (formerly The Swan with two Necks) in Westgate. Two seasons ago he was elected as a member of the Huddersfield C and AC Committee, and just more than 12 months ago he became a member of the Football Committee.

'The team that never kicks'

In an appreciation of Wagstaff, 'Rouge' some time ago wrote: "Every man in the side was a footballer of exceptional ability and unbounded enthusiasm. Thus, Wagstaff was extremely fortunate in having a machine which responded almost automatically to his ideas almost before they were formed; his comments appeared to be football Zancigs, so quickly did they read their captain's thoughts. The 13 was often described as "The team that never kicks". This was somewhat of a licence, but was fundamentally true, and doubtless was the result of a theory in which 'Waggie' was a great believer, vis: that possession was nine-tenths of the game, and it was foolish when you had it to present it to the opposition. Kicking was seen, of course. Both Holland and Gwyn Thomas used their feet at full-back and Wrigley was at times very effective in this part of the game. Then Rosenfeld was an expert in the short kick over and regaining possession, and Moorhouse was a past-master in the art of kicking inside. But taken as a whole the team may be said to have depended on their handling.

It was said that kicking was the only thing Waggie could not do. For my part I should not agree with this view, for I very much doubt whether anyone ever saw him try. A man who could dribble as effectively as he did must have had the ability to kick had he cared to cultivate it. His ball control was wonderful. Indeed, it was said of him that had he transferred his attention to the round ball he would have attained honours as high in the 'Soccer' world as those he gained in 'Rugger'.

In discussions concerning great players I have often heard men attempting to pick out outstanding features in Wagstaff's football. Not once have I heard a man succeed. This was not because there was nothing to get hold of. It was because there was so much that one could find nothing standing out above the rest. If in search of the secret of his success, the nearest one could get would be: 'Quick thinking combined with perfect technique'. No player ever demonstrated more thoroughly the importance of this split second in both attack and defence, and certainly none ever timed his efforts with greater success. So completely did he believe in the power of mind over matter that it was said of him that he never relied upon his weight and strength. This was true to a great extent, but when occasion arose Wagstaff made use of his splendid physique in a manner that would have done credit to Billy Batten."

Club testimonial
On the occasion of his retirement, the Huddersfield club presented him with the following testimonial:
Huddersfield Cricket and Athletic Club
A Tribute to Harold Wagstaff – a great rugby league footballer and a thorough sportsman

Dear Sir,
The Committee and all other members have pleasure in placing on record their deep appreciation of your invaluable services to the club throughout the whole of your lengthy and unrivalled football career.

At the early age of 15 years you were given a place in our first team, and from thence onward until your retirement from the game at the end of season 1924–25 your unexampled greatness in the football world gained for you every possible honour. In club, county and international games, you have had the privilege many times of leading your side to victory.

Your crowning honour came when you were elected captain of the British rugby league team which toured Australia in season 1914. Your success and popularity in the homeland was continued 'Down Under', and as a great player and captain you at once won the respect and admiration of the keenly critical colonial followers of the game.

Huddersfield people will always remember with great pride the fact that throughout your lengthy career not one single instance can be recorded against you of an action out of keeping with the great name you have made for yourself and the Club.

We appreciate the fact that you will always have the interests of 'Huddersfield' at heart and we can assure you throughout the remainder of your days that you will carry with you the best wishes of all at 'Fartown'.

We are, yours faithfully,
Joseph Turner – President
Arthur ET Hinchcliffe – Chairman of the General Committee
September 1925

Report of the funeral
Huddersfield Daily Examiner 22 July 1939

Harold Wagstaff laid to rest at Holmfirth
Former club-mates act as bearers
Large crowds watch cortege pass
Vicar and "a legendary figure"

Harold Wagstaff, "The Prince of Centres" and the former England and Huddersfield rugby league captain, was laid to rest today in Holmfirth Cemetery before a large gathering of sportsmen and friends.

On the coffin, which was of plain, unpolished oak, rested a wreath from "The Boys of the Fartown Football Team." This wreath took the form of a rugby football and was composed of gold tiger lilies and claret carnations tied with ribbons of claret and gold.

One of the mourners was Mr EV Booth of Holmfirth, who gave Wagstaff his first 'football' – a yeast bag stuffed with old rags. Mr Booth told an *Examiner* representative that when he was a youth working in a grocer's shop they used to play rugby with the old yeast bags and that was how Harold learnt the game. "When we had used all the bags at our shop we used to go and beg them from another grocer" he said.

The internment was preceded by a service at Holmfirth Parish Church. When the cortege left the Royal Swan in Westgate, Huddersfield, of which Wagstaff was the licensee, the street was crowded with sympathisers. Outside the Royal Swan people were standing 10 deep on the pavement, and the crowd stretched all the way down the street to Market Place.

It is estimated that 2,000 people saw the cortege leave for Holmfirth, and traffic in the centre of town was held up for a while. The traffic lights at the junction of Westgate and New Street were turned off and extra police were required to control the traffic.

The cortege was led through the town by a police car, and large crowds watched it go past. Large crowds also lined the road at Berry Brow and Honley to watch the cortege pass – a remarkable demonstration of public sympathy.

People began to assemble near the church some time before the service was due to begin, and when the cortege reached the entrance to the church, the pavements in the vicinity were crowded with sympathisers. Large crowds lined the streets to watch the cortege pass and in Victoria Street the crowd was particularly dense. Special constables assisted the regular police to control the traffic.

Eight of Wagstaff's old team-mates acted as bearers. They were Messers Douglas Clark, Winnpenny Brook, Arkle Hirst, Major Holland, Stanley Williams, Ben Gronow, William F Kitchin and George Todd.

"A legendary figure"

The service at the church was conducted by the Vicar of Holmfirth (the Rev TH Cashmore). In his address he referred to the fact that Wagstaff was a native of the town, but he had carried his name far beyond these hills and valleys. "He was an almost legendary figure in the particular sphere of sport in which he excelled" the Vicar said.

Wagstaff's family were very well known in the district and they had a special place in his (the Vicar's) affections and because of that he had a special interest in Harold Wagstaff. Wagstaff was also his brother in Masonry and he (the Vicar) knew how profoundly Wagstaff had strived to carry out the tenets of their craft.

A long list of the mourners was published. Alec Fiddes, the Huddersfield captain, represented the other players. Other clubs represented included Huddersfield Town AFC, Underbank (Holmfirth) RFC, Hunslet RLFC, Huddersfield Old Boys RFC, Halifax RL Club, Halifax RL Supporters Club and the Yorkshire Society of Referees. Wreaths were sent by the above clubs, and the Council of the RFL, Bradford Northern, Broughton Rangers, Yorkshire County RL and Wigan RLC.

The grave of Harold and Ann Wagstaff in Holmfirth Cemetery. The inscription reads: "In Loving Memory of Harold Wagstaff who died 19 July 1939 aged 48 years, also Ann his wife, who died 9 April 1955 aged 69 years."
(Photo: Peter Lush)

A Wagstaff Gate

"The popularity of footballers is fleeting", wrote a local contemporary following Huddersfield's first Yorkshire Cup victory, which was the prelude to their record breaking achievements in Northern Union football before the first European War. "The members of the team are now the idols of the hour. They had better make the most of it." It is only too true that public memory is both short-lived and devoid of gratitude. In the realms of sport, entertainment, and politics, the hero of one generation is quickly replaced by a new arrival who makes his bow before wildly cheering crowds. He in turn will make his exit and be forgotten as were those who appeared before him. Not all pass from the scene with the fruits of their triumphs to compensate them and mingle with memories of the days that will never return. For some the departure from the public scene is filled with tragedy. Happily during the last decade many of the men and women whose names have been on everyone's lips have made sensible provision for the time when they will no longer be able to command large fees.

    Because of the conditions under which rugby league football is conducted, few players are without a trade or profession. The big clubs have also taken steps to reward those who give loyal service over a long term of years. Soon, we hope, it will be obligatory on all club managements to say "Thank You" in this way to their players upon retirement. For those who wish to remain in the game, there should in the years ahead be an increasing number of openings for coaches, trainers, and managers. The ex-player who has no need to seek such employment can, however, serve his old club as a committee member, and many are already doing so. We are not so rich that we can afford to discard anyone who has a contribution to make to the game. It may be that a man will not always find his true vocation at the first time of asking, but trial and error must never be used as an excuse for refusal to experiment. Many of our best players have made their names in very different team positions to those they occupied upon their introduction to senior football.

    Having made certain the living are not forgotten, we can turn to those who, if they are absent in the flesh, are not easily forgotten because of their deeds. Few Northern League clubs have not the memory of some outstandingly great exponent of the code worthy of perpetuation at their grounds. The Wigan club's fine scoreboard was erected in recognition of the worth of two grand players – Jimmy Leytham and Bert Jenkins. Oldham hopes to rebuild one of their stands at Watersheddings and name it "The G.F. Hutchins Stand" in memory of a former long serving official. Now comes news of a proposed memorial to one of the greatest players who ever graced our game – certainly the greatest to wear the famous claret and gold jersey of the Fartown club – the late Harold Wagstaff.

To Mr Harry Sunderland must go the credit of first suggesting the memory of Wagstaff should be perpetuated at Fartown. We have not always found ourselves in sympathy with the various schemes propounded by this veteran of the game, but on this occasion we are in entire sympathy with his aim and wholeheartedly give it support. Towards the end of last June and during the English RL tour of Australia, the official opening took place by The Minister of Transport of new gates and turnstiles at Toowoomba Athletic Oval, the gift of Tom Gorman and E.S. Brown. Mr Sunderland was present at the ceremony, and made reference to "Waggy" and the match he played on the ground during the 1920 tour. His suggestion of a similar memento for Wagstaff at Fartown was well received by the Toowoomba League supporters. Within the space of a few minutes nearly £10 was collected to form the basis of an appeal fund. Friend Harry agreed to act as the custodian of the fund and promised to make a far-reaching appeal to all RL supporters and well-wishers.

The main entrance to the Fartown enclosure in Spaines Road is scheduled for extensive alterations by the Huddersfield Corporation when agreement is reached between the three committees concerned – Estates, Highways, and Passenger Transport. Now is the time to come forward with plans for a "Wagstaff Gate", and to invite all followers of the club to make donations to the Appeal Fund. Not only Huddersfield RL "fans" but those who revere the memory of "The Prince of Centres" will wish to be associated with this memorial. We do not know what arrangements Mr Sunderland has made to receive subscriptions, but we shall be pleased to open our columns to acknowledge their receipt. There should be no difficultly about the Huddersfield club giving its approval to the proposed memorial, for their esteemed president has in many speeches reminded members of the great and noble heritage of their club. Indeed, no man has been more zealous of the good name of Fartown sportsmanship on the playing field, both at football and cricket.

We hope that there will be an immediate response to Harry Sunderland's Wagstaff Memorial Fund, and that it will be possible to inaugurate the "Wagstaff Gate" at Fartown during this Festival Year. The memorial would serve as a reminder to all who visited Fartown of the honour which a local lad brought to the club and of his services to England, both at home and "down under". To the young generation who would walk through its portals it would bring a sense of realisation that they too could follow in his footsteps the paths to football glory. And even if they could not quite emulate all his playing feats, they could pursue the example of sportsmanship which he set throughout his whole career.

From *Rugby League Review*, edited by Stanley Chadwick, 12 January 1951.

NB A gate never was named after Harold Wagstaff at Fartown, nor was anything else. There is nothing named after him at the John Smith's Stadium either.

A 1922–23 Yorkshire team: Back: Major Cass, J. Betteridge (York), L. Marshall (Bramley), J. Wild (Wakefield T), P. Brown (Dewsbury), W. Batten (Hull), F. Gallagher (Batley); front: W. Clements (Featherstone R), Joe Lyman (Dewsbury), H. Wagstaff (Huddersfield), J. Brittain (Leeds), R.E. Turnbull (Halifax); kneeling: A.F. Binks (Leeds), L. Osborne (Hull KR).
(Courtesy Robert Gate)

Left: Harold Wagstaff and Billy Batten before their final appearance for Yorkshire against Lancashire at Oldham in 1923. Lancashire won 6–5.
(Courtesy Robert Gate)

Leadership

The 1914 'Rorke's Drift' test match win against Australia was "A triumph for teamwork if ever there was one – but a tribute to Harold Wagstaff's inspired leadership too.

It was that leadership that had, you know, its part in making Huddersfield into what was probably the finest of all club teams seen during rugby league's 68 years history. Of course, "Waggy" had at his command a dozen or more top class performers – forwards and backs alike of great power – but he led them with the touch of a master. He was the striking force in the famous "standing pass" movement that produced so many tries and which few teams in living memory have used to such profit. With his other ideas, his personal skill and his leadership he left an indelible mark on the 13-a-side code."

From *Harold Wagstaff* by 'Knightrider' – *Rugby League Magazine* Number 5, December 1963.

"Made captain of the Huddersfield team in September 1911 [age 20], his astuteness and strategy gained numerous victories for the side. During these years many bright chapters were added to the annals of the game by the teams which 'Waggy' so ably led. New moves were introduced, and the game which had been in the doldrums for several years after the turn of the century reached fresh heights."

A.N. Gaulton, *Rugby League Review*, 14 July 1950.

Huddersfield versus Wigan in 1948, showing the huge terrace at Fartown. (Courtesy *Rugby League Journal*)

Appendix: Harold Wagstaff's playing record
by Robert Gate

Huddersfield:
Debut 10 November 1906 at Bramley
Last game 23 March 1925 at Oldham

Season	App	Tries	Goals	Pts
1906–07	21	6	8	34
1907–08	24	2		6
1908–09	35	11	1	35
1909–10	5	1		3
1910–11	30	14	2	46
1911–12	40	21	1	65
1912–13	34	22		66
1913–14	30	16		48
1914–15	38	34		102
1918–19	1	1		3
1919–20	34	13		39
1920–21	27	6		18
1921–22	35	15		45
1922–23	18	3		9
1923–24	35	8		24
1924–25	29	2		6
Totals	**436**	**175**	**12**	**549**

Trophies won:
Challenge Cup: 1912–13, 1914–15, 1919–20
NRL Championship: 1911–12, 1912–13, 1914–15
Yorkshire Cup: 1911–12, 1913–14, 1914–15, 1918–19, 1919–20*
Yorkshire League: 1911–12, 1912–13, 1913–14, 1914–15, 1919–20, 1921–22
*Huddersfield won the Yorkshire Cup in 1909–10, but Wagstaff did not play in any of the matches.

Career record

	A	T	G	P
Huddersfield	436	175	12	549
Tests	12	2	-	6
England	9	7	3	27
Yorkshire	15	4	-	12
Representative games	4	-	-	-
1914 Tour**	9	11	4	41
1920 Tour**	9	10	-	30
TOTALS	494	209	19	665

**Excluding tests
***The records for the 1914 and 1920 tours of Australasia are incomplete.

Representative record

Tests (12)

Great Britain 10 Australasia 19	8 November 1911	Newcastle
Great Britain 11 Australasia 11	16 December 1911	Edinburgh 2 tries
Great Britain 23 Australia 5	27 June 1914	Sydney
Great Britain 7 Australia 12	29 June 1914	Sydney
Great Britain 14 Australia 6	4 July 1914	Sydney
Great Britain 16 New Zealand 13	1 August 1914	Auckland
Great Britain 4 Australia 8	26 June 1920	Brisbane
Great Britain 8 Australia 21	3 July 1920	Sydney
Great Britain 19 New Zealand 3	7 August 1920	Christchurch
Great Britain 11 New Zealand 10	14 August 1920	Wellington
Great Britain 6 Australia 5	1 October 1921	Leeds
Great Britain 6 Australia 0	14 January 1922	Salford

Internationals (9)

England 14 Australia 9	2 January 1909	Huddersfield
England 39 Wales 13	10 December 1910	Coventry Try, 2 goals
England 27 Wales 8	1 April 1911	Ebbw Vale Try, goal
England 6 Australasia 11	18 October 1911	Fulham Try
England 31 Wales 5	20 January 1912	Oldham Try
England 40 Wales 16	15 February 1913	Plymouth Try
England 16 Wales 12	14 February 1914	St Helens Try
England 33 Other Nationalities 16	5 February 1921	Workington Try
England 2 Wales 13	7 February 1923	Wigan

County games (15)

Yorkshire 30 Cumberland 0	17 October 1908	Huddersfield
Yorkshire 0 Lancashire 13	31 October 1908	Salford
Yorkshire 3 Lancashire 17	7 November 1910	Wigan
Yorkshire 13 Cumberland 16	9 December 1911	Millom
Yorkshire 12 Lancashire 13	25 January 1912	Halifax
Yorkshire 19 Cumberland 5	5 December 1912	Hull KR Try
Yorkshire 20 Lancashire 8	16 December 1912	Oldham 2 tries
Yorkshire 3 Cumberland 8	11 October 1913	Workington
Yorkshire 5 Lancashire 15	24 September, 1919	Broughton
Yorkshire 25 Cumberland 9	22 October 1919	Hunslet Try
Yorkshire 27 Cumberland 6	6 November 1920	Maryport
Yorkshire 8 Australians 24	7 December 1921	Wakefield
Yorkshire 9 Cumberland 4	28 October 1922	Maryport
Yorkshire 11 Lancashire 11	7 December 1922	Hull KR
Yorkshire 5 Lancashire 6	8 December 1923	Oldham

Bibliography by Graham Williams

Books

Billot, John — *All Blacks in Wales* (Ferndale, 1972)
History of Welsh International Rugby (Cardiff, 1999)
Chadwick, Stanley — *Claret and Gold 1895-1946* (Huddersfield, 1946)
Collins, Tony — *Rugby's Great Split* (London, 1998)
1895 and all that (Leeds, 2009)
Dalby, Ken — *The Headingley Story 1890-1955 Volume 1: Rugby* (Leeds, n.d.)
Davies, D.E. — *Cardiff Rugby Club: History and Statistics 1876-1975* (Cardiff, 1975)
Davis, Jack — *One Hundred Years of Newport Rugby* (Newport, 1974)
Delaney, Trevor — *The Roots of Rugby League* (1984)
Rugby Disunion Volume 1: Broken-Time (Keighley, 1993)
Dewhirst, John — *Room at the Top* (Shipley, n.d.)
Life at the Top (Shipley, n.d.)
Farmer, David — *The All Whites* (Swansea, 1995)
Haynes, John — *From All Blacks to All Golds* (Christchurch, 1996)
Gate, Robert — *Gone North Volume 1* (Sowerby Bridge, 1986)
Grant, Philip J. — *The Greatest Game Ever Played* (Neath, n.d)
Griffiths, John — *The Book of English International Rugby 1871-1982* (London, 1982)
Hammond, Dave — *The Club: Life and Times of Blackheath FC* (London, 1999)
Hardcastle, Andrew — *The Thrum Hall Story* (Halifax, 1986)
Harris, CRG — *The Statistical History of Cardiff RFC 1876-1984* (Cardiff, 1984)
Heywood, Brian, Sheard, Stuart, Smith, David, Thorpe, David
Standing on the shoulders of Giants (Huddersfield, 2015)
Hoole, Les — *The Rugby League Challenge Cup* (Derby, 1998)
Howitt, Bob & Howarth, Diane *1905 Originals* (Auckland, 2005)
Hughes, Gareth — *The Scarlets* (Llanelli, 1986)
Jenkins, John M, Pierce, Duncan, Auty, Tim
Who's Who of Welsh International Rugby Players (Wrexham, 1991)
Latham, Mike — *Buff Berry and the Mighty Bongers* (Chorley, 1995)
Leatherdale, Clive (ed) *The Book of Football* (Southend on Sea, 2005)
Marshall, Rev. Frank (ed) *Football: The Rugby Union Game* (London, 1892)
Matthews, Brinley E. *The Swansea Story* (Swansea, 1968)
McCrystal, John — *The Originals* (Auckland, 2005)
Moorhouse, Geoffrey *A People's Game* (London, 1995)
Morgan, W. John & Nicholson, Geoffrey *Report on Rugby* (London, 1961)
Morris, Graham — *100 Greats: Salford Rugby League Club* (Stroud, 2001)
Salford City Reds: A Willows Century (Skipton, 2002)
Rugby League in Manchester (Stroud, 2003)
The King of Brilliance (London, 2011)